A HISTORY OF
BLACK
AMERICA

A HISTORY OF
BLACK AMERICA

Dr. Howard O. Lindsey

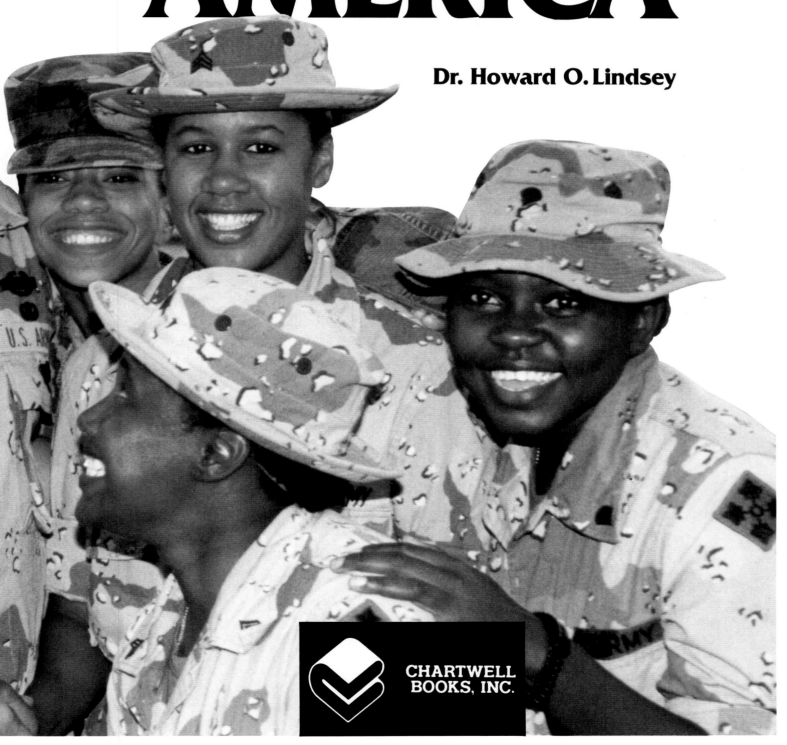

CHARTWELL
BOOKS, INC.

Acknowledgments

The publisher thanks the following individuals who assisted with the preparation of this book: Sara Dunphy, the picture editor; John Kirk, the editor; Ron Callow of Design 23; and Elizabeth McCarthy, the indexer.

Grateful thanks also to the individuals at the institutions and agencies cited below who kindly provided illustrations for this book:

Abby Aldrich Rockefeller Folk Art Center, Williamsburg, VA: page 38.

AP/Wide World Photo, Inc.: pages 137 (top), 145 (top right), 148 (bottom right), 150 (top left, bottom left), 151 (bottom left), 156 (bottom).

The Bettmann Archive: pages 1, 9, 11, 12 (top), 16, 19, 22, 23 (bottom left), 24 (both), 25, 33, 34 (bottom right), 40 (both), 41 (bottom), 42 (top), 46, 48 (both), 53 (both), 54 (all three), 55 (top), 60 (left), 62, 65 (bottom), 66, 67 (top), 73 (bottom), 76 (bottom left), 78 (both), 81, 82 (top left), 84 (bottom right), 88 (bottom right), 89, 90, 93 (both), 94 (top right), 95 (bottom right), 99 (top left), 101 (top left), 106 (bottom left, right), 107 (top right), 108 (bottom left, right), 109, 110 (bottom left), 113 (bottom), 114 (bottom right), 116 (bottom left),156 (top right).

Bettmann/Hulton: pages 12 (bottom), 17, 108 (top right).

Bison Picture Library: page 8.

The Boston Athenaeum, Boston, MA: page 82 (bottom right).

Bostonian Society: pages 27 (top), 55 (bottom).

The British Museum: page 15.

Brompton Picture Library: pages 35 (top), 56, 106 (top right), 157 (top left), 158 (top left, center left).

The Charleston Museum, Charleston, SC: pages, 6, 7 (bottom left), 23 (top right).

Chicago Historical Society: page 104 (top left).

Denver Public Library, Western History Department: page 97 (bottom center).

Duke Photo Department, Duke University, Durham, NC: page 149 (top left).

Malcolm Emmons: page 145 (bottom right).

Henry Ford Museum & Greenfield Village, Dearborn, MI: page 99 (bottom right).

Courtesy of the Hagley Museum & Library, Wilmington, DE: page 74 (bottom right).

Harvard University Archives, Cambridge, MA: page 98 (bottom left).

Harvard University, News & Public Affairs, Cambridge, MA: page 149 (bottom right).

Kansas State Historical Society, Topeka, KS: pages 64 (top left), 97 (top right).

The Library Company of Philadelphia: pages 50 (top right), 51 (bottom right).

Library of Congress: pages 20, 21, 29 (bottom), 31, 32, 41 (top), 42 (bottom), 43 (top), 47, 57 (bottom), 60 (top), 64 (top right), 65 (top right), 68, 69, 73 (top), 77, 79, 80, 88 (top left).

Lincoln University, Langston Hughes Memorial Library, Lincoln University, PA: pages 61 (bottom), 75 (top).

Louisiana State Museum, New Orleans, LA: page 83 (top).

Courtesy of the Lynn Historical Society, Lynn, MA: page 94 (top left).

Courtesy of The Mariners Museum, Newport News, VA: page 26 (bottom).

Maryland Historical Society, Baltimore, MD: page 39.

Massachusetts Historical Society, Boston, MA: page 26 (top left).

Metropolitan Museum of Art, Gift of Mr. & Mrs. Carl Stoeckel, 1897: page 63 (left).

Michigan State Archives, Lansing, MI: page 57 (top right).

Military Order of the Loyal Legion & the US Army Military History Institute, Massachusetts Commandery, Carlisle Barracks, PA: pages 72 (both), 85.

Minnesota Historical Society, St. Paul, MN: page 100 (bottom).

Mississippi Department of Archives & History, Archives and Library Division, Special Collections Section: page 76 (top right).

Missouri Historical Society, St. Louis, MO: page 61 (top).

Monticello, Thomas Jefferson Memorial Foundation: page 18 (top right).

National Archives: pages 67 (bottom), 74 (top, bottom left), 100 (top left).

National Museum of African Art, Smithsonian Institution, Washington, D.C.: pages 10 (both), 14.

National Museum of American Art, Smithsonian Institution, Washington, D.C./Art Resource: page 151 (bottom right).

National Portrait Gallery, Smithsonian Institution, Washington, D.C.: pages 82 (top right), 142 (top right).

Nebraska State Historical Society, Solomon D. Butcher Collection: page 97 (top left).

New Bedford Whaling Museum, New Bedford, MA: page 52 (top left).

New Hampshire Historical Society, Concord, NH: pages 70 (bottom), 71, 75 (bottom).

New York Public Library, Arents Collections, New York, NY: page 28.

Oberlin College Archives, Oberlin, OH: pages 44, 45, 50 (bottom left), 51 (top left, right), 63 (right), 96 (bottom left).

The Phillips Collection, Washington, D.C.: page 151 (top).

Enoch Pratt Free Library, Baltimore, MD: page 96 (top left).

Princeton University, Princeton, NJ: page 149 (bottom left).

Reuters/Bettmann Newsphotos: pages 2-3, 144 (bottom left, top right), 145 (top left), 147 (both), 152 (both), 153 (top left, right), 154 (bottom right), 155 (left center, bottom left), 157 (top right, bottom left, right), 158 (top center, bottom).

Schomberg Center for Research in Black Culture, New York Public Library: pages 106 (top left).

Courtesy of The Society for the Preservation of New England Antiquities, Boston, MA: pages 58, 59.

South Carolina Historical Society, Charleston, SC: page 49.

Courtesy Spelman College Archives, Atlanta, GA: page 95 (top left).

The Stowe-Day Foundation, Hartford, CT: page 86 (bottom left).

Swarthmore College, Friends Historical Library, Swarthmore, PA: page 50 (bottom center).

TV/Sports Mailbag: page 154 (bottom left).

UPI/Bettmann Newsphotos: pages 4-5, 7 (bottom right, top left), 18 (bottom left), 36, 95 (top right), 101 (top right, bottom), 102 (both), 103, 104-105 (bottom center, top right), 107 (bottom), 110 (top left), 111 (top left), 112 (top), 113 (top), 114 (top left), 115 (both), 116 (top right), 117-136, 137 (bottom), 138-139, 140 (both), 141, 142 (bottom left), 143 (both), 144 (bottom right), 145 (bottom center), 146 (both), 148 (top, bottom left), 149 (top right), 150 (bottom right), 153 (bottom), 154 (top left, right, bottom center), 155 (top left, right, bottom right), 156 (top left), 158 (top right, center right).

U.S. Department of the Interior, National Park Service, Edison National Historic Site: page 94 (bottom left).

The United States Military Academy Archives, West Point, NY: page 86 (top right).

University of Virginia Library, Tracy W. McGregor Library, Special Collections Department, Manuscripts Division: page 37.

Virginia Historical Society, Richmond, VA: page 34 (top left).

Virginia State Library, Richmond, VA: page 52 (bottom left).

Wadsworth Atheneum, Amistad Collection, Hartford, CT: pages 43 (bottom), 83 (bottom), 84 (top), 87, 91 (both), 92, 98 (top), 111 (bottom right), 112 (top right).

Weidenfeld Library: pages 13, 29 (top).

Western Reserve Historical Society, Cleveland, OH: page 70 (top).

Yale University Art Gallery, Trumbull Collection, New Haven, CT: page 35 (bottom).

PAGE 1: The revered Booker T. Washington, in about 1900.

PAGES 2-3: General Colin Powell, former chairman of the Joint Chiefs of Staff, visits U.S. troops during the war with Iraq in 1990.

PAGE 5: Mrs. Rosa Parks, whose defiance of segregated bussing in Montgomery, Alabama, in 1955 ignited the modern civil rights movement.

Published by
CHARTWELL BOOKS, INC.
A Division of BOOK SALES, INC.
110 Enterprise Avenue
Secaucus, New Jersey 07094

Produced by
Brompton Books Corp.
15 Sherwood Place
Greenwich, CT 06830

ISBN 1-55521-960-8

Printed in Slovenia

Contents

Introduction

The dictionary defines an odyssey as "a long wandering voyage usually marked by many changes of fortune." That is an appropriate definition of the history of people of African descent in the United States. Their voyage has certainly been long, and it could hardly have been marked by more dramatic changes of fortune.

Though Africans have been in the Americas since at least the time of Columbus, the story of Africans in North America begins in 1619, with the landing of the first contingent of Black settlers. The history of the African in North America thereafter is one of tragedy and triumph, the story of America at its worst and its best. Until the mid-nineteenth century it is a history dominated by the institution of slavery, even though much of that history was made by Africans who were

An urban kitchenhouse in Charleston, S.C. Slaves prepared meals here and carried them to the master's table in the main house.

not slaves. From the days of Reconstruction to the present it is the story of a long struggle to obtain justice – economic, social, political, and legal.

Black history is about the rural South and the urban North. It is about slave minstrels, Scott Joplin, Billie Holiday, Jackie Wilson, Michael Jackson, Prince, and L. L. Cool J. It is about Black horse jockeys at the first Kentucky Derby. It is about Frederick Douglass, W.E.B. Du Bois, Martin Luther King, Jr., and thousands more.

The United States is said to be a nation of people on the move, and this has been especially true of African-Americans. In few other groups have so many people moved to different parts of the country in such a relatively short period of time. The Great Migration saw people of African descent abandon the South in favor of the northern cities, changing aspects of their culture in the process. African-Americans now form the most urbanized population group in the country. The traditions of the Gullah-speaking people of the Sea Islands of South Carolina and Georgia have given way to "rap" and "hip hop" trends of the 1990s.

There have been great changes in the nation over the past three centuries. For African-Americans, a gauge of those changes was the transition from "property" to "personhood". Yet despite all the upheaval witnessed by Africans, they have managed to cling to some of their African ancestry. There is, for example, still a strong attachment to family. And the Black Church is still the most powerful institution in the community. But there can be no pretending that the Black community is still the relatively isolated and simply-structured thing it once was. It has grown from a few dozen persons to tens of millions, and today African-Americans are found coast to coast, in all 50 states.

With so much history and diversity to consider, it would be impossible to cover everything in one volume. This

LEFT: In 1966 Black freedom marchers carry a 106-year-old man on their shoulders as they go to register to vote in Mississippi.

LEFT BELOW: A basket woven from sweetgrass, one of the artifacts unique to the Gullah-speaking Blacks living on the Sea Islands off South Carolina's coast.

BELOW: Widow Coretta King and family at the 1968 funeral of the martyred Rev. Martin Luther King, Jr.

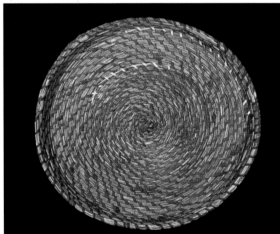

study is simply an attempt to introduce the reader to the history of people of African descent in America, and the writer is all too aware that much of significance has necessarily been scanted in this brief overview. Yet perhaps after examining this work the reader may have a better grasp of the history and culture of one of America's largest and oldest ethnic groups, and if this, in turn, may inspire him or her to do more reading about the subject, the efforts of those involved in producing this book will have been well rewarded.

Chapter One

The West African area where Atlantic slave traders were at their most active in the eighteenth century.

Most of the Africans who were caught up in the Atlantic slave trade came from West Africa, an area roughly from the Senegal River in the north to the Congo River in the south. While these Africans represented a number of different societies, languages, and religions, they shared many cultural traits, and some of the most fundamental of these can still be discerned in contemporary African-American culture.

The heart of all social, economic, and political life for most West Africans was the extended family. The core of such a family consisted of a father and his brothers, along with their families, but it also extended backward in time to include each man's father and his uncles, as well as their families. When a man and his wife had children, the sons would take wives, who would become a part of the extended family, and the

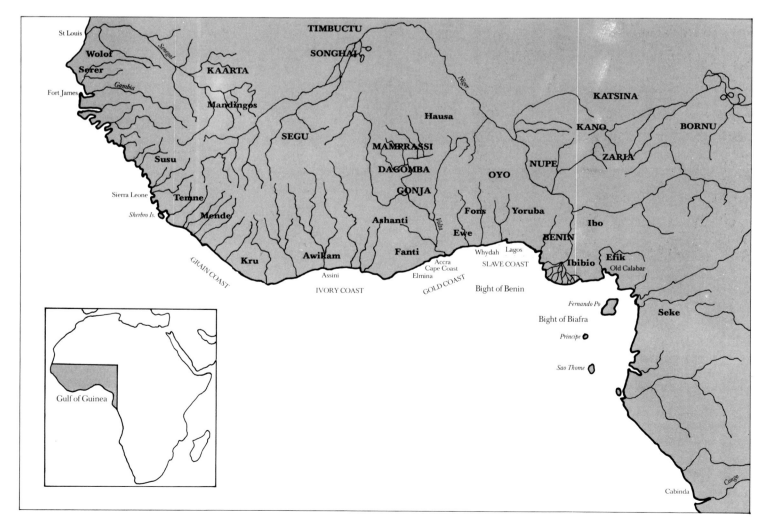

8

Africa Before the Slave Trade

daughters would leave home when they married to become a part of their husbands' extended families. Also part of every family were the spirits of all the deceased ancestors within the family's collective memory.

A family usually lived in a village composed of a number of other extended families. The families often shared the same lineage, *i.e.*, were presumed to have originated from a common blood ancestor. Several lineages, in turn, could form a clan, a group thought to be descended from a common "mythical" ancestor or dependent on the protection of a supernatural guardian.

Africans considered all adults responsible for all the children of the village, and, by the same token, children were expected to obey all adults as if they were their biological parents. This

The town of Cape Coast on the Gold Coast (of what is now Ghana) was one of the main slave ports operated by the Royal African Company, England's chief slave-trading enterprise in the eighteenth century.

The status of women in this patrilineal society was clearly subordinate, but it would be a mistake to exaggerate the degree of that subordination. Wives had clearly defined rights, and if they were violated, it was understood that the victims' families could and would seek vengeance. When a bride was chosen, custom demanded that the prospective groom give her family a "bride price." In effect, the husband's family was compensating the bride's family for losing so valuable a person. That women *were* uniquely valuable members of African society there was never the slightest doubt.

Traditional West Africans believed the spirits of dead ancestors, within collective memory of the village, could take actions that affected the living, and ancestral spirits were accordingly

ABOVE: A Beninese bronze-and-iron-inlay head made by craftsmen of the royal court in the fourteenth century. Known for its sculpture, the West African Kingdom of Benin existed from the thirteenth to the nineteenth century.

RIGHT: A nineteenth-century wood carving of a mother and child from the Congo-Zaire region. The fact that she wears a chief's cap is noteworthy.

communal emphasis on childrearing was at once cultural and practical. Daughters were essential to the survival of the race, sons would carry a family name into the next generation, and both were vital to a family's well-being. It was they who had to be counted on to look after the elderly when they became too old to support themselves. It was they who had to take over when a family member became sick, injured, or otherwise incapacitated. Their labor, in the house or in the field, increased the family's — and therefore the community's — wealth, and their members added to the community's ability to defend itself against outside attack. Small wonder they were cherished.

shown great respect, though they were not worshiped. They were thought to watch over the family and to protect it from unseen evil forces. But they were also thought to monitor the actions of all family members and to punish transgressions. Since an individual was simply a reflection of the collective family, the spirits might decide to punish either the offender or any other member of his/her family. The effect that this uncertainty had on fostering social order was considerable.

Another feature of African culture that promoted both social cohesion and social control was the system of "age grades." Individuals born within a certain cluster of years went through life together as a group, something like fraternities for the males and sororities for the females. The members would help one another in time of need — with labor, material goods, protection, counseling, and the like — and in return, all members were expected to abide by the rules of the group and could be punished for infractions. As an age grade advanced in years, its power and respect within the community grew, achieving its highest status when its members reached the rank of elders.

As a result of these various institutionalized social controls, crime in most traditional African societies was almost nonexistent, and so, consequently, was the need for punishment. Yet punishment did exist, and in some ways its most severe form was banishment from the family. Since Africans felt there was virtually no life outside the extended family, expulsion from it was considered to be on practically the same level as execution. For lesser offenses ostracism from the village community was the usual sentence. This was not as harsh as banishment, but it was nevertheless potent because it brought shame to the offender's family, something few Africans could bear to contemplate.

The African Economy

Most West Africans lived in small rural villages. They sustained themselves by growing food crops such as

yams and grains or by herding cattle and other livestock, with yields from fields and flocks being supplemented by hunting and gathering. Ownership of land was essentially communal, for West Africans believed that humans could not really "own" land, this being seen as the property of the Supreme Being. The lineage or clan, in the person of the "Master of the Ground," parcelled out available land on the basis of family size. So important was this function that the Master of the Ground often acted independently of any local political authority, even that of a king. Land was to be used and cared for in trust by the occupants, and abuse of the land would bring sanctions — mainly divine sanctions.

Yoruba farmers in what is now Nigeria gather to harvest durra, a staple grain sorghum.

RIGHT: An eighteenth-century engraving by a European artist who plainly knew nothing of Africa purports to show the costumes and architecture of Benin.

BELOW: Some examples of Beninese sculpture cast in bronze by the *cire perdue* process. The head is of an Oba, or King, and probably dates from the 1300s. The earliest surviving Oba heads go back to the twelfth century.

Even though people lived in fairly small, isolated areas, that did not mean that they had no contact with other people. Since their economy tended to produce surpluses, West Africans engaged in lively trading ventures with communities some distance from their own. This was done primarily via well established regional markets. At specific times people from the villages in a region could meet at certain fixed locations to exchange goods. This system permitted some villages to specialize in various economic activities such as metalwork, pottery, or woodcarving, allowing them to sell or barter such specialties for other goods or staples they might lack. Many markets were not exclusively regional. Knowing when and where markets would be held allowed traveling merchants to carry goods from great distances to trade and sell. It should also be noted that the merchants of the marketplaces were frequently women.

As important as markets were to the economies of the various peoples of a region, they served other vital func-

tions as well. They were places for learning news about other regions, places to socialize and meet friends and relatives, occasionally places to meet a prospective spouse. They were also places where disputes between clans and lineages could be settled. Quarrels among members of a particular village could usually be settled by a local council of elders, but in situations where a dispute involved a number of villages of different clans, any purely local council's ruling would be suspect. Thus men who had a wide reputation for settling disputes, or even a judge appointed by a king, would often travel with merchants from market to market, offering their negotiating services in ideally neutral territory.

Political Organization

At the village level, politico-judicial functions were mostly carried out by councils of elders. The decisions of these councils were seldom capricious, for they had to be firmly rooted in tradition and popular consensus and, in any case, had to be unanimous. Once

A photograph of a clan shrine in Mali. It is dedicated to a semi-mythical ancestor of the Keita clan named Sundiata, who is said to have founded Mali.

rendered, however, they became communal law.

Many villages were not part of any larger polity, but broader political institutions did exist, and the most grandiose of these were the kingdoms. Between AD 800 and AD 1600 three great kingdoms flourished in West Africa: the kingdoms of Ghana, Mali, and Songhay. All were located below the Sahara Desert and above the Gulf of Guinea, and the basis of power for all three was control of the trans-Sahara caravan trade. The major items traded were gold, wheat, textiles, leather, sugar, and, above all, salt. Most of the major trading centers were located near the desert, and one of the biggest problems facing these communities was food preservation. Salt was virtually the only commodity capable of preserving food, and especially meat, in a hot dry climate. It made possible the existence both of the trading towns and of the grueling trans-Saharan trade on which they depended. It was as valuable as gold and was often used in place of it as a medium of exchange.

The first of the great kingdoms to flourish before the rise of the trans-Atlantic slave trade, the Kingdom of Ghana probably occupied an area north of the present-day nation of Ghana. It had a strong agricultural base and used its surplus produce for trade. It thrived from AD 800 to shortly after AD 1000. Its fall was due mainly to the encroachment of the Sahara Desert – what had been farmland was claimed by the desert as the rains ceased and the topsoil eroded away. But the kingdom was also subject to Muslim invaders who harried it from the north.

Mali was the next great nation-state in the region. It was a Muslim kingdom under the control of the Malinke people. Like Ghana, it was a rich agricultural kingdom that controlled the trans-Sahara camel caravan trade. Its capital was Timbuktu, a cultural center and the site of Sankore University, specializing in Muslim law and medicine. (It is said that at the medical school of the university cataract operations on the human eye were routinely performed.)

OPPOSITE: A mounted clay figure from Mali. It may date from the tenth century.

ABOVE: A seventeenth-century Benin bronze statue of a Portuguese musketeer.

The most celebrated ruler of the empire was Monsa Musa (1307-1337), who gained fame throughout the Muslim world when he led a fantastic pilgrimage to Mecca in 1321. Supposedly the king took an entourage of over 20,000 civilians and soldiers across the Sahara Desert. Along the way he spent so much gold that the market for gold in Arabia was depressed for three years. Whether in spite or because of this, the empire began a rapid decline after Monsa Musa's death in 1337.

The last and largest of West African kingdoms before arrival of the Europeans was Songhay, which dominated not only the camel caravan trade but the water trade along the River Niger. Under its greatest ruler, Askia Mohammed, the kingdom reached its zenith of power, controlling a large part of sub-Saharan Africa. Its capital, Tim-

buktu, had an estimated population of 100,000. But in 1591 a Moroccan army, including European mercenaries equipped with guns, defeated the Songhay forces at Tondibi on the Niger River, and though the Moroccans never occupied the empire, the disaster was enough to cause Songhay's eventual political collapse.

Literature and Art

Although the Africans had a rich oral tradition of poetry, mythology, and history, most West African languages were not written down until the fairly late arrival of Islam and Arabic script. Indeed, those tongues not influenced by Islam would have to wait until the era of colonialism for the introduction of the written word. But much was preserved, all the same. Every lineage, clan, or village designated a group of

Ibo ceremonial masks in the Smithsonian Institution Museum's collection in 1931. Today the Smithsonian African collection is so big that it fills a separate museum — the National Museum of African Art — in Washington, D.C.

16

individuals as the keepers of the official history of the group. These people were called "griots" (It was griot whom Alex Haley used to verify his family history in order to write his epic work *Roots*.) Modern scientists have shown that the individuals who kept these oral histories could preserve them intact with astonishing accuracy, and it is on the dwindling ranks of today's griots that historians must now depend in their efforts to re-create in writing Africa's literary past.

In most African societies there was very little "art for art's sake." African art was usually functional, often serving religious or magical purposes. But it was no less powerful for that: indeed, its effect on European and American art in the past 200 years would be hard to exaggerate. Because African artists often worked with perishable materials such as wood and fabrics, relatively little of the art that exists today is of great chronological age. But it is almost all of great "historic" age, since in spirit and execution it faithfully adheres to artistic traditions that were old long before the slave trade even began.

The culture of the West Africans was both rich and diverse. It was different from European culture, but in no sense inferior to it. When the slavers came to West Africa, assaulting both the people *and* their culture, it was they who played the role of barbarians.

The slave trade would cause tremendous upheaval in the life and culture of traditional West Africa, but of course even more in the lives and culture of the West Africans brought to the New World in chains. The "Middle Passage" would involve millions of Africans in one of the most horrendous undertakings in human history. And one of its effects would be the creation of a new kind of human being: the African-American.

This bronze plaque from Benin shows two faces with curiously European features, perhaps Portuguese. The Portuguese first visited Benin City in the fifteenth century.

Chapter Two

BELOW: Probably the first Blacks in North America: indentured servants who landed at Jamestown in 1619.

RIGHT: Culture shock as symbolized in money: African cowrie shells and Spanish coins.

Contrary to popular belief, the first Africans in the New World were not slaves. Africans may, indeed, have been among the first people from the Eastern Hemisphere to visit the New World, for there is some evidence that Africans could have arrived in the Americas as early as the 1300s. Dr. Ivan Van Sertima speculates that Central America may have received African visitors during the era of the Mali Empire in West Africa. While the evidence is still a matter for debate, there is no debating the

African presence with Columbus, for when the Italian explorer sailed to the New World from Spain he had several Africans in his crew.

Nor were the first Africans to arrive in what would become the United States slaves: they were probably indentured servants, 20 of whom landed at Jamestown, Virginia, in 1619, a year before the Pilgrims reached New England. Slavery was not at this time even a developing institution, but already America was beginning to feel the urge to fill its most basic need, finding a cheap, reliable source of labor.

In 1619 the capacity of North America to generate wealth for Europe was only beginning to be appreciated. It did not seem to offer the same treasure trove of gold, silver, and other precious minerals that the Spaniards had found in the south, but no one could doubt its agricultural potential. Many valuable crops such as cotton, tobacco, sugar, and rice could not be grown on a profitable scale in Europe but apparently could be in the Western Hemisphere. Could be, that is, if a way could be found

Colonial America
1619-1787

to offset the high cost of transporting them, or their derivative products, back to Europe. The most obvious answer to that problem was to cut labor costs, cut them, indeed, to levels far below any then existing in Europe. But that could be done only if a large labor force of a wholly new kind could be found, and finding such a force was to be a major preoccupation of the North American colonists for the roughly 40-year period between 1619 and 1660.

The first group to which the North American colonies turned to fill their labor needs were the European (mainly British) poor, and the condition under which these poor Whites were brought to the New World can, in general terms, be described as indentured servitude. (Technically, the term embraces several categories — indentured servants, tenant farmers, redemptors, bond servants, apprentices, and so on — but all were similar in general form.) Typically, the system involved a colonist's paying the passage of someone

A slave auction on the African coast. The Atlantic slave trade burgeoned in the mid-1600s and continued to grow steadily into the nineteenth century.

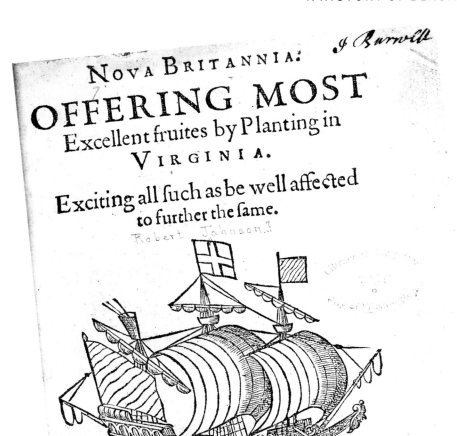

J. Burwell

NOVA BRITANNIA:
OFFERING MOST
Excellent fruites by Planting in
VIRGINIA.

Exciting all such as be well affected to further the same.

Robert Johnson.?

LONDON
Printed for SAMVEL MACHAM, and are to be sold at his Shop in Pauls Church-yard, at the Signe of the Bul-head.
1 6 0 9.

A recruiting poster from the earliest days of English settlement in North America. The settlers would soon be in desperate need of a source of cheap labor for their plantations, a need they would in time fill by enslaving African men and women.

from England or Europe to work in America as a servant, farm worker, or skilled tradesman. Before the European left home he would sign a contract specifying his duties, his term of service (usually seven years), and his compensation (usually very low). Once the parties agreed, the contract was often cut into two halves, the American employer keeping one part and the servant the other.

In theory it seemed like a fair and logical method to solve the labor problem. In reality the flaws of the system began to appear almost immediately. Even though seven years might seem a considerable time to spend as a servant, it was not long enough. If the

American employer had to train his servant in a trade, by the time the servant became fully proficient he was free. The labor force was not really permanent. Nor did it ever reach the numbers hoped for by the colonial authorities. Worst of all, it was not nearly cheap enough.

The system also laid the groundwork for future social troubles, though this did not become evident until later. Many of the people who came from England were young single males. They had envisioned working for a term of years and accumulating enough money and/or land to join the "planter class." For most, this never happened. Instead, the situation produced in some colonies groups of young, landless men with few prospects and a good deal of resentment against the society from which they were excluded. Inevitably, this led to various outbursts of violence, probably the most famous of which was Bacon's Rebellion in 1676.

Another group which the early colonists hoped might provide a source of cheap labor were the Native Americans, and many colonists experimented with Indian labor at one time or another. But the results were always disappointing. The most basic problem was simply that the New World Indians were not numerous enough to meet the enormous needs of colonial labor. And this was complicated by the fact of low Indian resistance to Old World diseases. A common Old World disease such as smallpox could wipe out whole villages once infection set in. Also, there was the problem of the whole tenor of Indian-colonist relations, which were at best uneasy and often degenerated into open warfare. From the colonist's point of view, the Indians always had to be thought of as potentially hostile. They could not easily be recruited for voluntary labor, and any attempt to make them work involuntarily stood a good chance of once again setting the tribes on the warpath.

Since the Native Americans could not be counted on to fill their labor needs, the colonists had to settle for taking away the Indians' land. There were in some cases treaties made with the

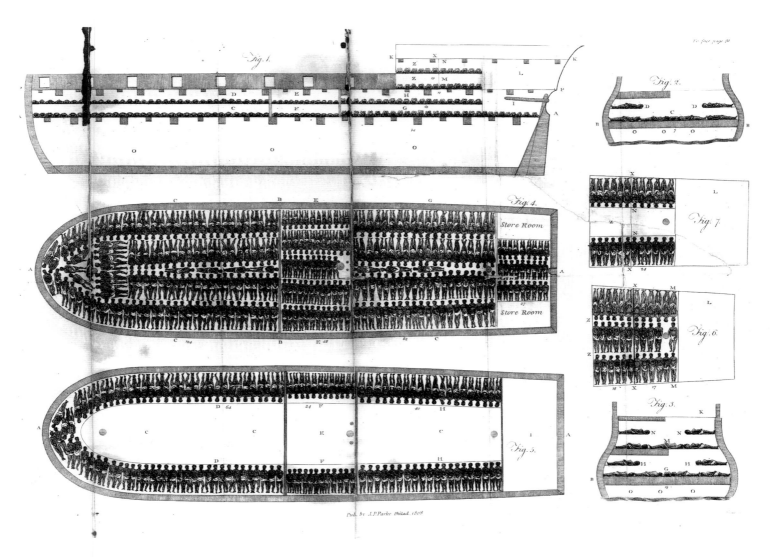

Fig. 1.

Fig. 2.

Fig. 4.

Store Room

Store Room

Fig. 7.

Fig. 6.

Fig. 5.

Fig. 3.

Pub. by J.P.Parke Philad. 1808

Native Americans to give the acquisition of their territory at least a quasi-legal basis. Even when the original treaties were broken (whenever it was convenient or profitable), they were usually replaced by yet other treaties or legal agreements. For the Africans, however, there would not even be the fiction of treaties.

The Rise of African Slavery

The idea that African slaves might be the answer to North America's labor problem dawned on the colonists only gradually – and, to their credit, some colonists, mainly in New England, refused to entertain the idea at all. But in purely economic terms, without reference to any moral considerations, the arguments in favor of such a solution were powerful. Unlike indentured Europeans or Indians, Africans were potentially in unlimited supply. As slaves, they would be as cheap as any

form of labor available anywhere in the world. At the same time, they represented a very high quality of labor, since most were already skilled farmers, stockmen, or artisans, understood the techniques of cooperative effort and division of labor, and were resistant to European diseases. Some of the crops and livestock that the African grew in his homeland were also grown in the New World. In fact, Africans probably taught the Europeans many techniques in cattle herding and in the cultivation of yams and grains.

One thing that made it easier for colonists to begin thinking of Africans as potential slaves was the perception that Africans had no real status under any legal system – national or international – that the colonists understood or, at any rate, were prepared to acknowledge. The African was not protected by recognized nation-states, as were most Europeans. Many people in

A cutaway plan of a "tight-packed" (see p. 29) slave ship. The ghastly "tween-decks" arrangement is all too well illustrated.

21

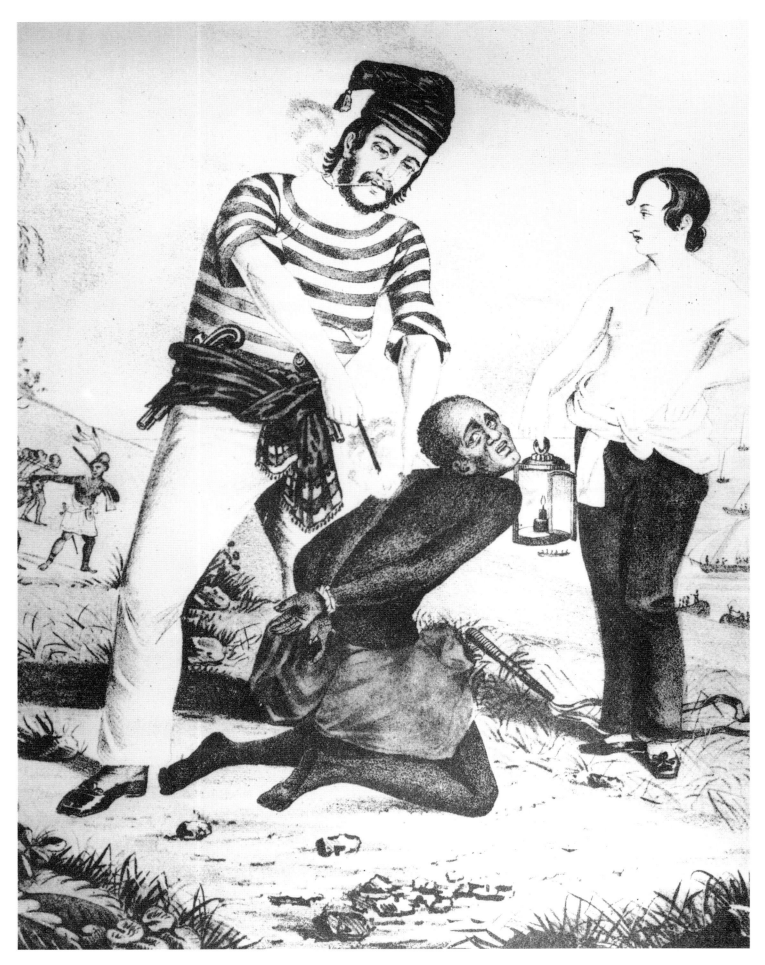

West Africa lived in small villages or clan groups, essentially stateless people who lived outside the rule of an all-powerful king. And from a practical military point of view, it would obviously be much easier to deal with small communities and villages than with a large centralized government possessing a standing army. Besides, the European superiority in weaponry could turn most battles in their favor, even though they might be vastly outnumbered by their adversaries.

The North American colonists' adoption of institutionalized slavery proceeded by gradual stages throughout the period between 1619 and 1664, when Maryland became the first colony to institutionalize slavery. At first, Africans were treated like any other indentured servants. Then, slowly, it became accepted practice for Black people to be held in servitude for longer periods than their White counterparts. Then Africans began to be classified as "servants for life." But even servants still had rights. The crucial last step that had to be taken was the destruction of those rights.

In what must be considered one of history's cruelest ironies, the first legal act in North America recognizing slavery was really intended to prevent its spread. When Massachusetts in 1641 enacted the so-called Body of Liberties, the legislators thought they were outlawing slavery, except under "certain circumstances," such circum-

stances including being a "lawful" war captive, voluntarily selling oneself into slavery, and so on. The "certain circumstances" enumerated in the Body of Liberties might seem so exceptional as to be relatively harmless, but the legislators had made a fatal error in allowing that there could be *any* circumstances in which slavery was legal. When other colonies, less opposed to

ABOVE: Slave tags issued in Charleston, S.C., show the date of issuance, the slave's number, and his/her skill.

LEFT: Slaves being readied for the trip to America, 1830.

OPPOSITE: Branding a newly-captured slave prior to embarkation.

RIGHT: The arrival of a new consignment of slaves in Charleston is advertised in an eighteenth-century handbill.

TO BE SOLD, on board the Ship *Bance-Island*, on tuesday the 6th of May next, at *Ashley-Ferry*; a choice cargo of about 250 fine healthy NEGROES, juft arrived from the Windward & Rice Coaft. —The utmoft care has already been taken, and fhall be continued, to keep them free from the leaft danger of being infected with the SMALL-POX, no boat having been on board, and all other communication with people from *Charles-Town* prevented.

Auftin, Laurens, & Appleby.

N. B. Full one Half of the above Negroes have had the SMALL-POX in their own Country.

BELOW: An 1835 bill of sale for the purchase of 10 Black slaves.

prevent the wholesale spread of slavery. And when legislation began to be enacted defining the legal status of the slave as "property," the last barrier preventing total exploitation was finally removed.

When the position of chattel slavery was formalized in the colonies something new was being created according to English law. When a colonial employer paid passage for a European to come to America, the European was not selling himself. What was being purchased and owned was the labor of the servant. The body of the servant didn't belong to his employer. But the chattel slave owned nothing. The master owned not only the labor of the slave but also his body. Not even the children of slaves belonged to their parents: slave children, too, could be bought and sold at the master's whim.

If there was any remaining doubt about the status of the slave as opposed to the servant, the early slave codes clearly illustrated the difference. Slaves were forbidden to carry guns in some colonies. They could not strike a white person. If a slave was caught stealing food, the punishment ranged from a minimum of 40 lashes for the first offense to death for multiple offenses. Early codes also required masters to search their slave cabins for weapons every 14 days. Slaves could not run away: by 1700 most of the colonies from Maryland to Georgia had adopted some form of special laws aimed at fugitive slaves. If they tried to escape, they could be hunted down. If a slave resisted capture and was killed, the owner could be compensated, and in some colonies public funds were used to pay for a slave killed "for good reason." Not that the "good reason" had anything to do with the rights of the slave: as early as 1669 the Virginia legislature had been the first to make it clear that it was not a crime to kill a slave.

the concept of slavery than Massachusetts, adopted similar legislation, they had no difficulty in so expanding the list of "certain circumstances" that within 24 years there was, in many colonies, hardly any legal barrier left to

Developing the Concept of Race

Removing legal impediments to the practice of slavery was one thing; finding moral justifications for the practice was another. How could one group of humans explain away their brutal exploitation of another group of humans as chattel slaves? The only possible answer was to deny that the subjugated group was fully human. It was not enough just to assert that African culture was inferior to European culture, since that implied that any Black who became acculturated in North America might become the equal of a White, thereby casting doubt on the propriety – even the legality – of the Black's slave status. For the slave system to work it was essential that Blacks be classified as innately, irredeemably inferior, members of a race destined by nature for subjugation. The distinctive dark skin of the African could then be seen not simply as the emblem of his race but of his sub-humanity.

That a doctrine so obviously dishonest and vicious should have gained such wide acceptance in the colonies, especially in the South, was a triumph of self-interest over morality, and even common decency. It was never, to be sure, a total triumph. The Quakers began their fight against slavery in Pennsylvania as early as 1688, and by the second half of the eighteenth century various other movements, such as the New York Society for Promoting Manumission, began to appear. In addition to such organized resistance to slavery, we can infer varying degrees of private resistance, both from the unequal distribution of the slave population among the colonies (*eg*, the 1790 census recorded 292,627 slaves in Virginia and 157 in New Hampshire) and from the small but steadily rising population of free Blacks in the second half of the eighteenth century (about 8.5 percent of the total African-American population by 1790). But the stark fact remains that almost nothing was done in *any* of the colonies to abolish the legal basis for slavery until a decade after the Revolution, and it would take another 80 years and a Civil War to eliminate the institution from the South. As for the lingering effects of the racial justification for slavery on the American psyche, they remain with us still.

In the best of worlds, the major Chris-

tian churches might have been expected to oppose both the spread of slavery and its racial justification. Converting non-Christian peoples to the True Faith was, after all, one of the Church's historic missions. Since biblical times, any convert who sincerely accepted the sacrament of baptism was understood to have been admitted into the Christian fellowship and to be, in God's eyes, on an equal footing with all other Christians. Discriminations made on the basis of race

The first European colonists to bring Black slaves to North America were the New Amsterdam Dutch, in 1646.

ABOVE: Cotton Mather.

BELOW: An eighteenth-century Virginia tobacco wharf.

had never been part of this process—indeed, could not have been, for that would have been at variance with the Church's universal proselytizing purpose.

Yet, with a few exceptions such as the Quakers, the colonial churches offered little doctrinal resistance to the rise of slavery. Not only did few churches protest when, between 1667 and 1671, a number of colonies enacted legislation stipulating that conversion by Blacks to Christianity could have no effect on their slave status, many prominent colonial theologians were already hard at work trying to find scriptural support for the racial argument for slavery. Thus Boston's famous Cotton Mather, in his 1693 work *Rules for the Society of the Negroes*, taught that slaves were the "miserable children of Adam and Noah" and that they should be faithful to their masters. In the catechism prepared for the slaves to memorize, Mather taught the Negroes that they

were enslaved because they had sinned against God and that it was God, not their masters, who had enslaved them. Service to the master was identified with service to God, and submissiveness to and respect for the master were equated with the similar deference which the owners gave to God. The Fifth Commandment (*Honor they Father and Mother . . .*) was twisted to mean for the slave, "I must show all due respect unto everyone, and if I have a master or mistress, I must be very dutiful unto them." The Tenth Commandment (*Thou shalt not covet . . .*) was interpreted as, "I must be patient and content with such a condition as God has ordered for me." For such compliance there would be little or no reward on earth, but, Mather assured his Black readers, God would prepare a mansion in Heaven for them where at last they would be "companions of angels in the glories of a Paradise."

Other ministers reiterated this

A MAP of the most INHABITED part of VIRGINIA containing the whole PROVINCE of MARYLAND with Part of PENSILVANIA, NEW JERSEY and NORTH CAROLINA Drawn by Joshua Fry & Peter Jefferson in 1775.

P O E M S

ON

VARIOUS SUBJECTS,

RELIGIOUS AND MORAL.

BY

PHILLIS WHEATLEY,

NEGRO SERVANT to Mr. JOHN WHEATLEY,
of BOSTON, in NEW ENGLAND.

L O N D O N:

Printed for A. BELL, Bookseller, Aldgate; and sold by
Messrs. COX and BERRY, King-Street, BOSTON.

M DCC LXXIII.

theme. In effect, Whites were being re-assured that God approved of slavery, and Blacks were being told that acceptance of slave status was a requirement for eternal salvation. It was not theology's finest hour.

The Slave Trade

In the sixteenth century the Portuguese became the first Europeans really to make a business of importing African slaves into the New World, Portugal's primary customer in this case being Spain, which was already beginning to be troubled by the dwindling supply of Indian labor in its South and Central American colonies. By the early seventeenth century the Dutch were competing with the Portuguese in this lucrative trade (the Dutch imported the first Black slaves into the principal Dutch settlement in North America, New Amsterdam, in 1646). The British had thus far held aloof from slave-running, but this was to change in 1672 when the Royal African Company was formed and was granted a monopoly of the English slave trade (the King was one of the Company's major shareholders).

At first, the Royal African Company's efforts were mainly directed toward supplying African slave labor to work on the sugar plantations in the British West Indies, but by the 1690s the North American colonies were also beginning to emerge as important customers. How important is suggested by the fact that a rising chorus of complaint from would-be private traders in both England and the colonies finally forced the withdrawal of the Company's monopoly in 1698.

Once the slave trade was opened to free enterprise, the North American slave population soared. As an example, Virginia held 12,000 slaves in 1708, 23,000 in 1715, 42,000 in 1743, and 259,230 in 1782. As early as 1708 the Black population of South Carolina

ABOVE: Poet Phillis Wheatley (c.1753-84) was one of the most famous of all eighteenth-century American slaves. Her poems were published in London in 1773.

A TOBACCO PLANTATION

had already surpassed that of the White – a condition that would continue until after the Civil War – and by the 1760s South Carolina was importing African slaves at the rate of 2,800 each year. By 1790 well over one-fifth of the whole population of the United States would be enslaved.

The slaves were overwhelmingly concentrated in the agrarian Southern colonies, where their labor would be of the greatest value: 86 percent of all American slaves were held in North and South Carolina, Virginia and Maryland alone, whereas all of New England held considerably less than one percent. But this should not be taken to mean that New England had no economic interest in slavery. On the contrary, it was maritime New England that was the very lynchpin of the booming American slave trade. Boston, Massachusetts, and Newport, Rhode Island, were not only America's leading ports of departure for slave ships, they were for most of the eighteenth century the principal ports of entry for new slaves. Not far behind them in the pursuit of profit from commerce in human beings were Providence, Rhode Island, Portsmouth,

New Hampshire, and New London, Connecticut.

Slaves came to the colonies via two routes. Some were shipped to the colonies from the West Indies as excess cargo, but most, perhaps 85 percent, came directly from Africa. The majority were from West Africa, from between the Gambia River on the North and the Congo/Zaire River on the South, and slavers roamed as far as 300 miles inland to purchase or capture their human subjects. But because of early disputes, some North American slave ships also sailed around the Cape of Good Hope in order to procure bondsmen from the East African coast.

The horrors endured by the Africans in their transatlantic voyage into slavery have often been described but can probably never fully be grasped. Though many details of this infamous "middle passage" were vividly reenacted in Alex Haley's famous television series *Roots*, even this grim depiction had to be sanitized to allow it to be broadcast into the homes of millions of Americans, both Black and White. The summary comments which follow, though factual, are no better able to convey the whole truth.

Roughly speaking, the slave shippers fell into two groups: the "loose packers" and the "tight packers." The distinction had solely to do with profitability. The loose packers held that allowing some room for the Africans to move about and breathe would lead to less wasteful loss of life, even though this meant fewer bodies per square foot of space. The tight packers crammed their ships to overflowing, arguing that though more would die, enough would usually survive to bring a better profit than if they had been less densely crowded.

Such debates can have made little difference to the slavers' wretched human cargo. Most of the time, slaves were placed side by side like rows of cordwood, chained to each other and to the ship. Perhaps the least fortunate were those stowed in the "tween-decks," artificial decks built between two existing decks to maximize space; here, where the clearance might be as little

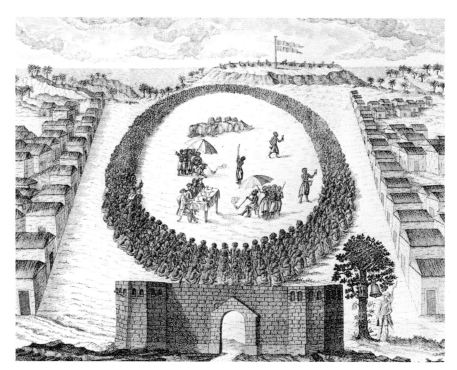

OPPOSITE: Relations between England and the American colonies began to sour afer the end of the French and Indian War (1763), when England tried to pay off its war debt by devising new taxes for the colonies. In this scene Bostonians in 1765 burn papers rather than pay duty on them, as required by the new Stamp Act. The coming revolution in America would, at least in the North, help to improve the status of some Blacks.

as 18 inches, death by asphyxiation was an ever-present possibility. About the best any of the captives could hope for was constant good weather and strong winds to make the journey as short as possible. Good weather might also mean that the cargo would be allowed outside on the open deck for short periods of exercise, for this tended to lessen the chances that its value would be depreciated by outbreaks of disease. But if the weather was bad, or if the Africans showed signs of rebellion, no such indulgences were granted. Worse, rough seas meant that entrances and air inlets to the cargo holds might have to be covered, raising the danger of suffocation to those on the tween-decks, and even on the regular cargo decks. Many who did not succumb went mad. And even in fair weather, the stench of sweat, blood, excrement, and decaying corpses in the cargo hold often made the members of the crew nauseous: sailors reported that they could stand being below deck for only short periods of time, even covering their mouths and noses.

The best time for a slaver to arrive in Africa was during the winter months, when contagious diseases spread less rapidly. The best time to arrive in America was between April and November, when demand for slaves was highest. The first colonial slave ships, which set out during the 1680s, could carry about 200 people. These ships were simply cargo vessels which had been fitted with temporary platforms to increase load capacity. Later, ships were built expressly for carrying human cargo. Bigger and faster, they could hold as many as 400, with a crew of 47. The average length of the voyage was 40-60 days. The per capita price for slaves rose steadily throughout the colonial period, as it would continue to do until the Civil War.

The duties that African slaves performed, once delivered to their colonial masters, ran practically the entire spectrum of occupations. In agriculture, slaves raised livestock, made dairy products, and cultivated tobacco and, later, cotton. In industry, they worked at shipbuilding, lumbering, metallurgy, distilling, carpentry, tannery, and so on. Those in skilled trades such as tailoring, blacksmithing, or printing tended to fare best, since they were the most difficult for their masters to replace. In all the colonies slaves also served as house servants, cooks, coachmen, and nursemaids.

Manumission and Free Blacks

As slavery developed into an institution, it became ever harder to free slaves, especially in the Southern colonies. The regulations governing the granting of freedom to the slave, manumission, varied from region to region. New York, for example, required that a master freeing a slave post a bond of $200 and pay the freedman $20 a year to insure the freedman would not become a burden on the colony. Other colonies imposed similar restrictions.

Manumission was not the only means by which Blacks could escape from slavery. Africans who had been indentured servants might eventually win their freedom, and a few Northern colonies, such as Rhode Island, set legal limits on how long a term of slavery could last. There was also the possibility of private agreements between the master and slave for freedom, usually involving the slave purchasing his or her freedom. In some cases, slaves won freedom through service in the colonial militia. Sometimes, old, infirm slaves were liberated simply because they were no longer productive.

There was, moreover, an increasing number of White individuals and organizations opposed to the institution of slavery itself. Few demonstrated more anti-slavery fervor that the Quakers, one of the few groups to base its anti-slave position on moral grounds. By 1758 the Quaker authorities had made it mandatory for all Quaker slave-owners to free their chattel, but in fact, Quaker opposition to slavery had by then been in existence for some 70 years and had succeeded in making Pennsylvania the most anti-slave colony of the colonial era. In 1780 the colony passed the first statute of the century calling for gradual emancipa-

tion. While this was a good sign, the law had little effect to those who were already slaves, for freedom was not to be granted to those who were slaves, but to their children. Even then, freedom was granted only upon their 28th birthday, after serving the mother's master for that period.

The Quakers apart, much colonial anti-slave sentiment was rooted in economic rather than moral concerns. White skilled tradesman, artisans, and laborers often became anti-slave simply because they found that they could not compete with slave labor. Despite demeaning racial stereotypes, it became clear early in the development of slavery that slaves could in fact perform virtually all the same tasks as White laborers. But by the same token, so could free Blacks. Emancipation was thus only a partial answer to the White workers' complaints and left in place the seeds of much future race-based tension.

There had always been small free Black communities in every colony throughout the colonial era. By 1790 there were only about 60,000 free

Blacks in the whole country. But because slavery was increasingly associated with race, many free Blacks found barriers in their quest for full citizenship rights. Even in New England, where there was never a large number of African-Americans, free or slave, laws placed limits on the freedom of non-slave Africans. Restrictions on free Blacks included denial of the privilege to serve on juries, lack of voting rights, and inability to own certain types of property. In some cases, free Blacks were even required to be off the streets after dark, or to have a pass in order to leave the towns in which they lived.

The American Revolution

By the middle of the eighteenth century it was becoming obvious that the relation between England and her thirteen North American colonies would have to be redefined. As the century progressed, the colonists grew ever more restive about their lack of representation in the face of taxation and complained ever more bitterly about how England was abridging their

ABOVE: An ex-slave, Crispus Attucks (1723-70), an early martyr of the American Revolution, was killed by British troops in the Boston Massacre.

OPPOSITE: The Marquis de Lafayette, ardent French supporter of the American rebels, was an opponent of slavery. His Black servant, shown here, used his master's noble family name.

ABOVE: The colonial governor of Virginia (1770-76), Lord Dunmore, tried to enlist Blacks in the British army to fight the rebel colonists. This act prompted the colonists to rethink their opposition to admitting Blacks into their own forces.

RIGHT: Declaration of Independence author Thomas Jefferson, by Rembrandt Peale. The Declaration avoided mention of the subject of slavery.

soon call the "Boston Massacre." Since this incident was one of the proximate causes of the Revolution, it is fair to say that one of the first casualties of that Revolution was an individual born in bondage. But would Attucks, or his descendants, be able to partake of the precious "freedom" for which he had given his life?

One of the first answers to that question is to be found – or, perhaps more significantly, is *not* to be found – in the colonists' great revolutionary manifesto of 1776, the Declaration of Independence, written and largely conceived by Virginia slave-owner Thomas Jefferson. Jefferson was in fact conflicted in his personal feelings about the institution of slavery and was violently opposed to the slave trade, but when he tried to insert language in the Declaration blaming England for initiating "this execrable commerce," Southern delegates to the Continental Congress objected and forced the language to be stricken. The result was that this second most famous of

legal rights to freedom and equality. Liberal democratic theoreticians such as Thomas Jefferson, Thomas Paine, and Samuel and John Adams generalized these grievances into matters of universal principle, thus helping to lay the intellectual foundations not only for a revolution but for the kind of egalitarian government it was meant to produce. In all this ferment, however, neither the theoreticians nor their less articulate colonial contemporaries paid much serious attention to the troublesome question of Black emancipation.

On March 5, 1770, five years before the War for Independence began, an ex-slave named Crispus Attucks and four White protesters were killed by British troops in what the colonists would

American documents did not really address the question of slavery at all.

Yet by not protesting against slavery while simultaneously asserting "that all men are created equal," the Declaration seemed to be making a sinister im-

34

plication: that the term "men" did not include Black slaves, that the Africans were simply not human, and therefore that the doctrines embodied in the Declaration did not apply to them. This implication may have had more long-range negative affects on the republic than was ever imagined in 1776.

The first shots of the Revolutionary War were fired at Lexington, Massachusetts, on April 19, 1775, when British General Gage fired upon a group of 70 colonial militiamen on the village green. Black men had been a part of the colonial militia forces since 1774, and African-Americans participated in all phases of the Revolutionary War, sometimes as slaves and sometimes as free men. Yet despite the obvious advantages to the American colonies of being able to draw on a pool of Black fighting men, Africans were not universally welcomed in the colonial armed forces. In fact, early enlistment of African-Americans was banned by George Washington in July 1775. This applied both to slave and free and came in spite

of the participation of Black soldiers in the opening battles of Lexington and Concord in April of 1775, and in spite of the fact that ex-slaves Peter Salem and Salem Poor had distinguished themselves at the subsequent Battle of Bunker Hill (unconfirmed reports suggest that Peter Salem may have shot English Major Pitcairn).

The prohibition on further enlistment of African-Americans might have

ABOVE: *The Declaration of Independence* by John Trumbull.

BELOW: John Trumbull's painting of the death of patriot Joseph Warren at Bunker Hill. Also fatally wounded (center) is British Major John Pitcairn, said to have been shot by patriot ex-slave Peter Salem.

ABOVE: Jefferson's home, Monticello, with the slave quarters in the foreground.

OPPOSITE: Like Isaac Jefferson, shown here in an 1845 photo, many ex-slaves adopted the surnames of famous American leaders. The irony of some of the choices was usually not understood.

remained in effect had it not been for an English colonial official. In November of 1775 the royal governor of Virginia, John Murray, Earl of Dunmore, authorized the enlistment of slaves into the British army, promising freedom to any slave or indentured servant who joined the British ranks. Though the number of slaves who joined with the British was not large, the prospect of a possible mass slave uprising against the colonists sent alarm throughout Virginia, and Dunmore's name was vilified more than even the king's. The most significant effect of Dunmore's maneuver was the lifting of the ban on Blacks enlisting in the Colonial forces.

Throughout the war slaves, ex-slaves, and free men of color found their way into all areas of the Continental armed forces. Some served in all-Black units, but the majority served and fought with White colonists in mixed companies. African-Americans also proved their mettle in the colonial navy, where they served as seamen, gunners, and even pilots. Some Blacks had piloted coastal vessels before the war, and their knowledge of off-shore waters proved invaluable.

The military phase of the Revolutionary War ended, for most practical purposes, in 1781, with the surrender of British General Cornwallis at Yorktown, Virginia. By this time nearly 300,000 men had served in the armed forces of the new nation, and of that total almost 5,000 were black. The Black soldiers and sailors won praise, and in some cases their freedom. A number of ex-slaves who had fought with the British also received their freedom, and some migrated to England with the withdrawing British troops. For the remainder of the people of African descent in America there was still the hope that the high-minded ideals of the Declaration of Independence, combined with gratitude for the services rendered by Blacks, would cause the new nation to rethink its commitment to slavery. Unfortunately this was not the case.

Chapter Three

A dance in the slave quarters of a Southern plantation, depicted by an unknown artist *c.* 1795. Many of the details shown — the musical instruments, women's headdresses, etc. — are clearly West African in origin (Yoruban, in fact).

Between the end of the war and 1786 the new United States struggled to find an identity under the loose provisions of the Articles of Confederation. But an insurrection in Massachusetts in 1785-86 over questions of debts and taxes prompted Americans to wonder if a stronger federal government might not be needed. In 1787 the leaders of several states invited all the states to send delegates to Philadelphia to draw up a new governing document. The delegates met from May 25 to September 16, 1787, and by June 1788 enough states had ratified the Constitution for

it to take effect. America now became the world's foremost laboratory for the practice of democracy. It did not, however, thereby become the world's foremost laboratory for the nurture of freedom and equality.

Whatever else it may have done, the Constitution sealed the fate of Black slaves in America for approximately the next 80 years. Unlike the Declaration of Independence, the Constitution did not simply ignore the institution of slavery; on the contrary, it was all too specific on the subject. The Constitution alludes to slavery in three places: twice

Growth of the Nation
1781-1865

in Article 1 and once in Article IV. It is worth looking at each of these passages in turn, for not only do they tell us much about prevailing attitudes in America in the late eighteenth century, they were to have powerful effects on the course of American history for a very long while.

Article I, Section 2, Para. 3, states: "Representatives and direct taxes shall be apportioned among the several States which may be included within this Union, according to their respective numbers, which shall be determined by adding to the whole number of free persons, including those bound to service for a term of years, and excluding Indians not taxed, three fifths of all other persons." This is the famous, or infamous, "Three-fifths Compromise" demanded by the Southern States, where the slave population was large. The passage has been misinterpreted to mean that slaves were to be counted as "three-fifths" of a person, but that is not what the passage says, nor is it really the point. What the passage says is that in each state only 60 percent (three-fifths) of the number of resident slaves will be counted for

The McCormick Family by Joshua Johnston (1765?-1830). A Black freedman, Johnston was the most famous African-American artist of his time. He specialized in painting portraits of wealthy Baltimore (Johnston's hometown) social leaders.

RIGHT: Eli Whitney working on his cotton gin. This 1793 invention, which made it possible for one person to produce 50 lbs of cleaned cotton a day, transformed Southern agriculture and hugely increased the demand for slaves.

BELOW: Free Black Benjamin Bannaker (1731-1806), a famous scientist of his day, helped to lay out the blueprint for Washington, D.C.

the purpose of taxation and representation, as opposed to 100 percent of the resident Whites. The following example may help to explain the political and economic implications of the formula.

Assume, for the sake of argument, that each state gets one representative to the House of Representatives per 1000 people. Assume also that property is taxed at rate of $100 per $1000-worth of property. Thus a non-slave state with a population of 7,000 people and property valued at $100,000 would be entitled to seven representatives in Congress and would have to pay $10,000 in property taxes every year. For a slave-holding state, however, the situation would be more advantageous. Let us say that such a state had a population of 10,000, half free and half slave. Let us also say that the state owned property valued at $100,000, with half of that total represented by the value of

the slaves. Thanks to the formula, the 5,000 free residents would get to elect (the slaves had no voting rights) not five but eight representatives to Congress and would have to pay not $10,000 in property taxes but only $8,000. Our hypothetical non-slave state might be annoyed by the inequity of this arrangement, but it had to bow to reality: such a compromise was better than giving the slave state 10 representatives and, in any case, accepting it was probably a price that had to be paid in order to get the Southern states to ratify the Constitution at all. But who was really paying the price, now that slavery had been acknowledged as an acceptable condition by the supreme law of the land?

The Constitution's second reference to slavery appears in Article I, Section 9, Para. 1. It states: "The migration or importation of such persons as any of the States now existing shall think proper to admit, shall not be prohibited by the Congress prior to the year one thousand eight hundred and eight, but a tax or duty may be imposed on such importation, not exceeding ten dollars for each person." However opaque the language of this passage might seem to some modern readers, no delegate to the Constitutional Convention had any doubt as to its meaning. Free people may migrate or immigrate to the country, but only one kind of person is "imported," and only that kind of person could be subject to an import tax, which is, after all, a kind of tax on a commodity. The Founding Fathers were talking about slaves and the Atlantic slave trade. They were sanctioning the continuance of this vile trade for at least 20 years (until 1808) and perhaps thereafter, if Congress so wished. They were also sanctioning, as they had in Section 2, the institution of slavery itself.

The final passage, Article IV, Section 2, Para. 3, declares: "No person held to service or labor in one State under the laws thereof, escaping into another, shall, in consequence of any law or regulation therein, be discharged from such service of labor, but shall be delivered up on claim of the party to whom

such service or labor may be due." Simply put, this is a fugitive slave law, a law ensuring that an escaped slave going to a "free" state would not automatically become free. Once again, the reasoning was based not on human rights but on property rights. A cow that crosses a state line is still the property of the original owner, and that property can be reclaimed upon production of proof of purchase or ownership. The same now applied to a slave, presumably also a non-human item of property.

The Founding Fathers had had a chance to strike a blow against tyranny, oppression, and bondage, to declare the end of slavery with a stroke of the pen. Instead, they gave the institution of slavery a new lease on life. In so doing, they introduced into what was otherwise one of history's most majestic documents a kind of deadly time bomb. By not confronting the issue of slavery with statesmanship in 1787, they condemned a later generation to confront it with guns and swords in a civil war that would come close to destroying the nation.

The Cotton Gin and the Rise of the Plantation System

At the time the Constitution was being ratified there were at least at few reasons for anti-slavery optimists in the North to hope that Black slavery in America might eventually wither away. The cost of maintaining slaves was

ABOVE: The murder of a free Black in the South is depicted in this 1817 Northern lithograph.

LEFT: Eli Whitney's cotton gin is so famous that history has virtually overlooked his other inventions, such as this milling machine.

RIGHT: An 1860s photograph of a slave family picking cotton in Georgia.

BELOW: Slaves loading cotton into a cotton gin.

rising, the soil in many slave states was slowly losing its fertility, and the South's main cash crop, tobacco, was fetching dwindling prices on the open market. It was just possible that the day might come when slavery would no longer be a paying proposition.

A Northerner named Eli Whitney inadvertently changed all that. In 1793, when he was visiting a plantation in Georgia, he saw slaves working on a crude machine that separated the seed from the cotton fiber. Whitney took this primitive device, made some improvements, and produced the "cotton gin," an invention that made it possible for cotton to be processed far faster and more cheaply than ever before. Almost overnight cotton began to replace tobacco as the South's great cash crop, and the demand for both more land and more slaves skyrocketed. Because the design of the cotton gin was so simple, Whitney couldn't control its manufacture, even though he held the patent. Thus Whitney never made a fraction of the money he thought he would, but he had nevertheless transformed both the economy of the South and the institution of slavery.

As cotton became "king," slavery truly entered the "plantation era." Large plantations were now not only feasible but immensely profitable. And the profits were not confined just to the South; the North benefited also, for slavery more than ever provided maritime and maritime-related jobs. As the demand for slaves rose, so did the fortunes of the New England slave traders, and New England shipowners filled the

seas with merchant vessels loaded with slave-grown cotton bound for the mills of England. When Congress "closed" the slave trade in 1808, as was now permitted under the Constitution, it was little more than a gesture. Slavery and the slave trade had become so profitable that even the most hopeful abolitionist knew that it would be a long time indeed before America could expect to rid itself of this hideous institution.

The rise of the plantation system also

TOP: Slaves aboard the Spanish slaver *Amistad* rebel and take control of the ship in 1839. Captured by a US Navy ship, the rebels were freed by U.S. courts.

ABOVE: Leader of the *Amistad* rebellion, Joseph Cinque.

43

In Oberlin, Ohio, in 1858, 20 abolition-minded citizens defied federal officers who were trying to return runaway slave John Price by abducting the fugitive. The rescuers were arrested, and the trial that followed became a *cause célèbre* in the North. The 20 are shown here in the yard of the Cuyahoga County jail.

had some important effects on the development of African-American culture. In former times, when the ratio of slaves to masters had been lower, relations between the two groups had been somewhat more personal, and a certain amount of cultural exchange had been possible. But the advent of the plantation system introduced slaveholding on a scale so vast that owners inevitably tended to lose human contact with all but a few individuals in their growing legions of slaves. As a result, the cultures of the two groups began to diverge more sharply than ever before, a fact that would have an effect on race relations in the United States for many years to come.

The new slave-quarters culture being created was a blend of African and European cultures, tempered by the constraints of American slavery. Far from being an attempt to duplicate the culture of the master, it was, in many

instances, the result of a conscious effort by the slaves to put as much cultural and psychological distance between themselves and the ruling White population as was possible under the circumstances. In certain "Black Belt" areas of the South that distance could be considerable. Perhaps the most extreme example was to be found on the isolated offshore islands below Charleston, South Carolina, where the Africans developed what was called the Gullah Culture. The heart of this culture was a unique language called "Gullah," a blend of English and several African dialects. But, as was the case in other emergent slave cultures, there was much more to Gullah Culture than just language. It produced highly specific customs relating to marriage, social relations between the young and their elders, polite modes of address, religion, and much else, and these customs were essentially expressions of something deeper, a view of the world that was not necessarily incompatible with the White worldview but was nevertheless different from it.

Resistance

Africans never submitted willingly to enslavement, and their resistance took many forms, ranging from outright rebellion and acts of sabotage to work slow-downs and running away. Even small acts of noncompliance served to heighten their sense of escape from their condition. Theft from the master was probably the most widespread form of passive resistance. In fact, according to the value system of slave culture one could only "steal" from another slave. Taking from the master wasn't really stealing but was simply a matter of taking back what had already been stolen.

By far the most popular form of active resistance for slaves was running away. This was, however, never easy. A slave rarely traveled great distances from the plantation, and not knowing exactly how to travel north only made the attempt more hazardous. There were also many practical questions involving procuring food, shelter, and hiding places along the way. If the attempt failed, and the runaway was captured, he or she would probably face very harsh punishment. On the other hand, successful escape could expose the runaway's family to punishment, since many slave-owners used this threat as a deterrent. In any case, running away meant leaving family and friends, not just temporarily, but probably forever. This was something that slaves with highly developed family ties and responsibilities found very difficult, and is part of the reason why so many of those who escaped were young, single males.

The dangers and complexities of the escape route to the North are matters to which we shall return later in this chapter when we discuss the Underground Railroad. But we should point out here that not all escaped slaves went north. Some became "Maroons." More common in Caribbean and South America, these were escaped slaves who lived in remote areas where civil authority was weak. They survived by living off the land and by occasionally raiding plantations for goods. Other escaped slaves, especially in Georgia, Alabama, and Florida, found friendly Indian villages which took them in and offered them shelter. A famous case of this kind occurred in the Everglade swamps, near present-day Miami. An escaped slave woman was taken in by the Seminole Indians, and she eventually married a young warrior named Osceola. The woman was later captured and re-enslaved by slave catchers. When Osceola, now a chief, demanded her return he was refused. His rage at this rebuff was one of the contributing

Some of the "Oberlin 20" were Black. One, John Scott, a former slave, is shown here with his family.

The fugitive slave laws were tightened in 1850, and Northerners showed their anger by organizing "rescues" of various fugitive slaves to block their being sent back to their owners. Here, a runaway named Thomas Sims is spirited out of Boston aboard the brig *Acorn* in 1851.

causes of the Second Seminole War, which raged from 1835 to 1842 and cost the U.S. government perhaps $60 million and the lives of about 2,000 of its soldiers.

The most serious form of slave resistance was, of course, revolt. Whenever one mentions slave revolts in the United States the names of three men stand out: Gabriel Prosser, Denmark Vesey, and Nat Turner. In 1800 Gabriel Prosser reportedly organized nearly 1,000 slaves in a planned attack on the city of Richmond, Virginia. His plans were thwarted by a sudden violent thunderstorm and betrayal by two slaves. Prosser, as well as nearly three dozen other African-Americans, were eventually tried and executed.

Denmark Vesey, unlike Prosser, was a freedman, having purchased his liberty in 1800, but he nevertheless vowed to strike a blow against slavery via armed insurrection in Charleston, South Carolina. He planned his uprising for a number of years and finally settled on a date in July of 1822. Unfortunately, his plot was discovered before it came to fruition, and Vesey

and a number of his co-conspirators were eventually caught, tried, and put to death.

Nat Turner's rebellion actually materialized. In 1831 Turner was a slave preacher in Southampton County, Virginia, who felt he was divinely inspired to take up arms to gain freedom for himself and his fellow bondsmen. After a sign from heaven, Turner commenced his revolt on August 21, 1831, and by the following day 60 White people had been executed by Turner and his followers. As the main body of slaves continued to march through the region they were engaged by federal and state troopers. Over 100 slaves were killed, but Turner managed to escape into the nearby swamps. He eluded capture for almost three months. During this period rumors that he had been sighted in every Southern slave-holding state spread panic throughout the South. Turner was finally captured in October 1831 and was executed the following month.

Turner's rebellion was merely the most violent expression of the universal phenomenon of slave resistance. It could never be said of any slave, even the most passive, that he did more than *comply*. None was ever *reconciled* to his lot, sentimental White Southern mythology notwithstanding.

Urban Slavery in the South in 1865

Not all bondsmen lived on rural plantations. By 1820 Black people averaged about 20 percent of the population of Southern cities, and in some cities, in-

CAUTION!!
COLORED PEOPLE
OF BOSTON, ONE & ALL,

You are hereby respectfully CAUTIONED and advised, to avoid conversing with the

Watchmen and Police Officers
of Boston,

For since the recent ORDER OF THE MAYOR & ALDERMEN, they are empowered to act as

KIDNAPPERS
AND
Slave Catchers,

And they have already been actually employed in KIDNAPPING, CATCHING, AND KEEPING SLAVES. Therefore, if you value your LIBERTY, and the *Welfare of the Fugitives* among you, *Shun* them in every possible manner, as so many HOUNDS on the track of the most unfortunate of your race.

Keep a Sharp Look Out for KIDNAPPERS, and have TOP EYE open.

APRIL 24, 1851.

A poster circulated by Boston abolitionists in 1851 warns Blacks (and, by implication, Whites) that the city police can no longer be trusted to ignore the fugitive slave ordinances.

By Jacob Radcliff Mayor, and Richard Riker Recorder, of the City of New-York,

It is hereby Certified, That pursuant to the statute in such case made and provided, we have this day examined one certain Male Negro Slave named George the property of John Delany

which slave is about to be manumitted, and he appearing to us to be under forty-five years of age, and of sufficient ability to provide for himself we have granted this Certificate, this twenty first day of April in the year of our Lord, one thousand eight hundred and fourteen

Jacob Radcliff

P. Riker

Register's Office Lib no 2 of Manumissions page 62
W T Slocum Register

cluding Richmond, New Orleans, and Savannah, Blacks actually outnumbered Whites.

African-American slaves performed many tasks in cities, from the hard, dirty work of porters and firemen to such highly skilled duties as those of bookkeepers and carpenters. But by far, most urban slaves were domestic servants: most middle-class urban families had at least one or two slaves. But though numerous, such servants were not used to produce wealth, as were the fieldhands on plantations; rather, they were luxuries and status symbols, showing that their owners had reached a certain level of affluence.

More significant was the work that urban slaves performed in industry. Richmond, Virginia's, tobacco industry was dominated by slave labor. According to author Richard Wade, Richmond's tobacco processing factories were so famous that they became tourist attractions, drawing crowds of visitors to see the slaves convert raw material to finished product. Until the Civil War, Richmond's ironworks also successfully used slave labor in many skilled and unskilled positions. The steel produced there was of a quality as high as any produced by free White labor in the North.

Other Southern cities also used slave labor in industrial positions. Richmond, Louisville, and New Orleans used slave labor in cotton mills. Charleston, Savannah, and Mobile used slave labor in the rice mills and on public works projects such as street and bridge repairs.

Hiring-out was a practice that greatly expanded the uses to which urban slaves were put. There never seemed to be enough slaves for all who wanted or needed slave labor, and if a slave-holder had any excess slaves, he could rent them out for a good profit. Hiring out could last for a day, a few days, or weeks and could involve many masters and a variety of jobs. "Hiring-out stations" were set up at various sites where slaves and employers could negotiate deals. The cities even issued licenses and permits to regulate the practice. Hiring-out was always good business policy and was especially useful for seasonal work, where more labor might be needed to perform specific tasks for short periods. Like all commodities in a free market economy, prices for renting slaves varied from city to city and depended on the skill levels needed for the tasks.

The nature of urban slavery had some unanticipated side effects that touched almost every slave living in a city. For one thing, it tended to put a premium on literacy. House servants, since they did the shopping, had to be able to read street and store signs and the labels of products; and of course they had to know some mathematics in order to make sure the master received his correct change. Slaves who hired out usually fetched higher prices if they were literate. Whereas rural slave-holders generally considered slave literacy as both unnecessary and something of a threat, the very nature of urban life fostered it, regardless of

any misgivings that owners might have.

Another side effect of city life was the emergence of what might be called "the quasi-free slave." At times some slaves found their work *without* the help of the master. These slaves contracted for jobs, negotiated a fee, and then paid their owners a fixed sum every month. With the money that was left over the slave bought his own food, clothes, and shelter. He rarely saw his master except on the days when he paid his master the fixed charge. In such cases the relations between master and slave began to blur into that of employer and employee. For the owners of such slaves, this situation was especially profitable, since they were relieved of the cost of having to provide food or shelter for the slaves. But by the same token, the "quasi free" tended to grow tired of paying masters who did nothing for them. When slaves could no longer reconcile the contradictions, they had two choices. One, the more dangerous, was to stop paying the master and try to relocate: in effect, run away. The other alternative was for the slave to negotiate a price with his master to purchase his freedom. Since many slaves

RIGHT: Even before the term "Underground Railroad" was coined, Quaker Isaac Hopper of Philadelphia was helping runaway slaves elude capture, work he began in 1787.

were skilled laborers, they could in fact accumulate the money to "purchase themselves," and some masters found their offers too good to refuse.

In balance, then, the extension of slavery into cities tended to be subversive of the whole system. How subversive is suggested by various facts and figures relating to the free Black community. From approximately 60,000 in 1790, the free Black population of the U.S. shot up to 488,009 in 1860, about 11 percent of the total Black population. And in every state save North Carolina, this free Black population was overwhelmingly located in cities: over 55 percent of Louisiana's free Blacks, for example, lived in New Orleans alone, and the 26,000 freedmen who lived in Baltimore constituted the largest free Black community in the nation. While it is undoubtedly true that freedmen tended to gravitate to cities, there is no escaping the parallel truth that cities tended to produce freedmen.

RIGHT: Abolitionist Levi Coffin, one of the chief organizers of the Underground Railroad.

BELOW: First president of the American Anti-Slavery Society, New Yorker Arthur Tappan (1786-1865).

Abolitionists

Though they usually fought a losing battle, the free Black population was in the forefront of the movement to end slavery. In some cases this was not solely a matter of altruism. Many free Blacks had relatives who were slaves. Also, they knew that as long as slavery existed, free Blacks would probably never be granted legal equality with Whites. But above all was the conviction that it was morally wrong to hold human beings in bondage. Free Blacks and ex-slaves were constantly protesting against the institution of slavery, as did a growing number of sympathetic White people who took up the cause to rid the nation of chattel slavery. But the fight for the abolition of slavery was to prove a long one, and in the end, victory would be achieved not by persuasion but at gunpoint.

As we have seen, there had been organized anti-slavery movements, Black and White, in America throughout the eighteenth century, but they had for the most part been small and scattered, and the most effective such effort, that led by the Quakers, had

been essentially confined to Pennsylvania. Though the anti-slavery crusade continued to grow in net size during the first two decades of the nineteenth century, it was not until free-Black and White abolitionists finally joined forces in a meaningful way in the 1830s that the movement at last became national in scope. The result of this coalition was the American Anti-Slavery Society, established in 1833. Among its Black founders were Robert Purvis, James McCrummell, James Barbadoes, and John B. Vashon, and it would very soon enlist such outstanding Black talents as those of Frederick Douglass, David Walker, Highland Garret, and David Ruggles. Among the leading White founders of the Society were Charles G. Finney, Theodore Weld, Arthur and Lewis Tappan, William Lloyd Garrison, and (a little later) Wendell Phillips.

The long-term goal of the Society was the complete and compulsory abolition of slavery everywhere in the United States. Its principal means to this end was what we should today call "consciousness-raising" – making White Americans fully aware not only of the moral evil of the practice of slavery but also of the racist lies that were used to justify it. By 1840 it had been sufficiently successful in this endeavor so that some Society members began to wonder if the time was not ripe to move beyond persuasion to more direct forms of political action. On this question the membership split, the activist going off to form a new organization (the American and Foreign Anti-Slavery Society), which in turn soon developed into a national political party, the Liberty Party. Whether this move into national politics was premature (as the "persuasionists," or Garrison wing of the original American Anti-Slavery Society, argued) is difficult to judge. Certainly the Liberty Party soon became an important force in American politics, but along the way, through the inevitable processes of compromise and courting of new constituencies, it probably lost a little of the focus and clarity of purpose that had been the strength of the original A.A.S. In 1848 the Liberty Party merged with the Free-

PAUL

CAPTAIN

CUFFEE

1812.

ENGRAVED FOR ABRM. L. PENNOCK, BY MASON & MAAS.

ABOVE: Paul Cuffee (1759-1817), an advocate of repatriating Blacks to Africa.

BELOW: African emigrant Joseph Roberts (1809-76), president of Liberia.

chief targets was the American Colonization Society, a group dedicated to repatriating Blacks to Africa, which he claimed was one of the worst enemies of Black Americans. He also chided African-Americans for not getting more involved in the abolitionist movement, and to this extent he might be considered an early "Black Power" advocate. Delany later served as an officer in the Union Army during the Civil War.

David Walker was a free Black living in the North. In 1829 he stunned the nation with the publication of a pamphlet entitled *David Walker's Appeal*, in which he charged that African-Americans were the most oppressed and degraded people in all of World History. The reasons he cited were: 1. Slavery; 2. Ignorance; 3. Christian ministers; 4. The African colonization movement. But his most controversial statement was that slaves should use violence to free themselves from bondage, that slaves should "kill or be killed in the pursuit of freedom." Needless to say, this sent shock waves throughout the slave states. The book was banned in the South, and Blacks, free or slave, could be punished if caught with a copy. Several slaves states even tightened their slave codes in response to the book. The following year, 1830, David Walker died under mysterious circumstances.

Probably the most famous female abolitionist was Harriet Tubman. She was also the most famous and successful "conductor" on the Underground Railroad. Tubman was born a slave in Dorchester County, Maryland, but made her escape from slavery in 1849. She soon decided that she should use her skills to help other slaves escape to freedom in the North or Canada. She returned to the South at least 19 times and led over 300 runaways to freedom. Shrewd and clever, she was never caught and never lost a "passenger." This was all the more remarkable because as her reputation grew she had a large bounty placed on her head, payable upon her capture. When the Civil War began she continued her heroic exploits by becoming a spy for the Union behind Confederate lines.

Soil Party, and thereafter its members became increasingly preoccupied with the more specific — though highly charged — question of whether new states being admitted to the Union should be slave or free.

One of the most important achievements that the abolitionist movement performed was to make White Americans aware of some of the truly extraordinary African-Americans who existed in their midst. There is hardly space in this book even to name them all, let alone provide their biographies, but a brief description of five of them may convey something of the quality of the group as a whole.

Martin R. Delany was a Black physician and abolitionist who had studied at Harvard Medical School. He criticized many White abolitionists for their own racist ideas, and one of his

Another noted female abolitionist was Isabella "Sojourner" Truth. She was born a slave in 1800 in Ulster County, New York, and was freed when the state outlawed slavery in 1827. She was a tireless advocate of both abolition and women's rights, including their right to vote. She gained national fame from her eloquent speeches against slavery and, perhaps as well, from her rather imposing physical presence. When she was 60 and living in Washington, D.C., she often walked to places she had to go rather than ride the segregated Washington streetcars. Sojourner Truth died in 1883 at the age of 83. She was buried in the city of Battle Creek, Michigan.

Frederick Douglass was probably the most famous of all the Black abolitionists. He had been born a slave in Maryland. Thanks to the wife of his owner, he learned how to read and write. This knowledge ultimately helped him to escape when he forged a pass to board a

steamship in order to flee his Maryland home.

He became an early follower of White abolitionist and publisher William Lloyd Garrison, and later, in 1847, he founded his own anti-slavery publication the *North Star*. By 1851 he had split with Garrison on the question of whether violence could be used as a tool for liberation. Though White and Black abolitionists both wanted to see slavery end, they often differed on tactics, and Black abolitionists tended to look not just at the problem of slavery in the South but also at the economic

ABOVE: The most famous Black abolitionist of all: Frederick Douglass (1817-95).

ABOVE RIGHT: William Lloyd Garrison (1805-79), Douglass's White counterpart.

RIGHT: An illustration from *The Emancipator*, one of the several abolitionist journals of the 1830s and 40s.

plight of African-Americans in the North. (They noted that there was rampant economic discrimination in the North and that even many White abolitionists failed to employ Black people in their businesses and in their anti-slavery activities.) But probably the most fundamental difference was the question of who should run the abolitionist movement, Blacks or Whites? This issue even split the Blacks, one faction remaining loyal to people like Garrison, who favored non-violent tactics and moral persuasion to end slavery, while others, such as Douglass, Delany, and Walker, advocated political action, and violence if necessary, and felt that Black people should lead the Black liberation struggle.

During the Civil War, Douglass worked to have Blacks admitted into the Union army and eventually helped to organize two Black Massachusetts regiments. He continued his fight for equality and civil rights through the Reconstruction period and, indeed, for the rest of his life, becoming the most respected African-American of his age and the recipient of many honors and government appointments (his last major post, 1889-91, was that of U.S. Minister to Haiti). He died in 1895. *The Life and Times of Frederick Douglass*, the final, revised edition of his autobiography, is a classic of its kind.

The Underground Railroad

Parallel with the abolition movement, and many ways more directly activist, was the increasingly organized effort to assist runaway slaves to escape to freedom in the North. In time, this enterprise came to be called the Underground Railroad. The term referred not, of course, to a real railroad but to the carefully planned escape routes the runaways could follow to the North or to Canada. The people who led the slaves out of the South were called "conductors." The "stations" were safe houses, barns, or other places where slaves could be hidden. The people who ran the "stations," called "station masters," provided food, shelter, clothes, and money to help the escaped slaves along the way.

ABOVE: A five-year-old slave child adopted by Catherine Lawrence, a Brooklyn, N.Y., matron, in 1863.

LEFT: Lewis Haydon (1815-89), a prominent Boston abolitionist, was elected to the Massachusetts state legislature in 1873.

Though all the people who participated in running the Underground Railroad did so at risk, the risk was incomparably greater for Blacks. Conductors such as Harriet Tubman had prices on their heads, and if caught would probably have been executed in the South. The station masters, usually free people who believed that slavery was wrong and wanted to do something about it, were free Blacks as well as White people. They, too, ran the risk of stiff fines, jail sentences, and mob violence. Slaves who escaped, either with or without the guidance of a conductor, also took great risks. If caught, they would almost certainly be punished according to the whim of the master. Even if a first attempt resulted in only comparatively mild punishment, subsequent unsuccessful attempts would probably lead to mutilation or death as an example to other slaves.

The escape routes followed roads, rivers and streams, and paths, often leading through woods and over mountains. In the East, many routes led to Philadelphia, which was just up the Delaware River from the slave states of Delaware and Maryland. In the Midwest, Cincinnati became a focal point for escapees. Slaves who continued north to Canada from these two routes usually crossed the Great Lakes at Buffalo, New York, or at Detroit. The railroad operated until the end of slavery in 1865. No accurate records exist as to the number of slaves who used this method to obtain their freedom, but the best estimates place the numbers at between 40,000 to 100,000.

The Northern Scene, 1800-1865

The Northern states, after most abolished slavery, were a common destination for escaping slaves: if there was no slavery in the North, then life had to be qualitatively better. But the slaves' perception that a Black person could be truly "free" in the North was often doomed to disappointment. In some Northern states African Americans were restricted in almost every area of life, either by law or custom, and discrimination and segregation were ram-

Henry (Box) Brown escaped from slavery, via the Underground Railroad, by being shipped North in a merchandise crate. He spent 26 hours in the 3×2½×2-foot wood box.

part. But at least conditions varied from state to state, and sometimes within states from one region or city to another.

Many Northerners feared that freed slaves would compete with Northern Whites for jobs and would depress wage scales, and it was in states with the highest free Black population, such as those bordering slave states, that residency restrictions tended to be most severe. Though not always enforced, African-Americans were usually required to post a cash security bond before they could settle in parts of some Northern states. In theory, this would limit settlement by African-Americans, since the bond would be set so high that few if any could afford to post it. If a Black person got into trouble with the law, the bond was forfeited. On the other hand, if the African-American decided at a later date to leave the area, the bond was returned. The system was plainly a contradiction of the American ideal of freedom of movement.

In Ohio, which had enacted a bond re-sidency law in 1829, the city of Cincinnati was especially fearful that large numbers of ex-slaves might decide to settle in the city. It therefore passed a series of additional "Black Laws," hoping to discourage Black migration. Apparently that was not enough. Mounting concern produced a full-scale riot in 1829, and the ferociousness of the melee reportedly drove away nearly half the Black population of the city. Many fled north to Canada and founded several communities in the province of Ontario.

This was not an isolated incident. Between 1832 and 1849 Philadelphia saw no less than five race riots initiated by Whites against Blacks.

The city of Detroit also experienced a violent slave-related incident in 1843. The episode involved a fugitive slave named Crosswhite, who had escaped and settled in the city. At the time there were only about 600 Black people in Detroit's population of approximately 40,000. Slave catchers from the escapee's home state of Kentucky captured Crosswhite and attempted to return

ABOVE: The subject of violent resistance to runaway-slave catchers in Detroit in 1843, David Crosswhite.

BELOW: An anti-slavery meeting on the common of Worcester, Massachusetts.

him to the South. Blacks in the city attacked the slave catchers and local sheriff and seized the ex-slave, who was then spirited across the Detroit River to Windsor, Ontario, in Canada. At the time almost 30,000 Blacks lived in the Windsor area, and they made it clear to Detroit officials that any attempt to cross the river and retrieve the fugitive Crosswhite would be met with armed resistance. The incident sent shock waves through the municipal government. The Detroit city fathers responded to this act of defiance by deciding they needed a "first line of defense" in case another incident of this kind occurred, and the event thus helped to spark the founding of the city's police force.

In most Northern states African Americans were barred from jury duty, and in some cases it was illegal for an African-American to testify against a White person. Other factors also prevented Blacks from obtaining equal justice under the law. For example,

Blacks could be arrested for certain crimes such as vagrancy, while Whites could not. African-Americans often could not get witnesses to testify on their behalf or afford the cost of competent legal help. They tended to be given longer prison terms than Whites for the same crimes and found it more difficult to get pardons. The mere fact that they had a harder time paying fines meant that they went to jail more often. The antebellum-North was, in short, still a long way from the promised land for free Blacks.

Dred Scott Case, 1857

Not quite half a decade before the start of the Civil War, any doubt that the spirit of slavery was not alive and well was destroyed by the infamous Dred Scott Case.

Dred Scott was a slave in the state of Missouri. His master took him first into Illinois and then Wisconsin before returning to Missouri. A group of abolitionist lawyers thought they could use

Dred Scott as a case to argue that since Scott had been taken into free states, his servitude had automatically been terminated, based on the provisions of the laws that had established Illinois and Wisconsin as "free-soil." Lower courts, including the Missouri Supreme Court, rejected Scott's plea, and the case finally ended up in the United States Supreme Court in 1857. Chief Justice Roger B. Taney and a majority of the other justices also rejected Scott's plea for freedom. That in itself was not surprising, given the times and circumstances, and if the ruling had just limited itself to this point it would not have been given much additional attention. But in their comments about the case (*obiter dicta*), the Democrat justices on the Court went far beyond denying Scott his liberty. Speaking for them, Justice Taney declared that Dred Scott could not bring suit in federal court because he was a Negro, not just a slave. In Taney's view, no Negro, whether slave *or* free, could ever be considered a citizen of the United States within the meaning of the Constitution. Thus Scott's real problem was not his servitude but his race. He was, in effect, subhuman.

In truth, Taney was merely stating as a principle a viewpoint that was widely put into practice on a de facto basis. Free Blacks had suffered under the yoke of slave codes in the South along with bondsmen. In the North they suffered discrimination in almost all facets of life, including the legal system. But now the highest court in the land seemed to be giving Constitutional sanction to practices that might not previously have stood the test of law, had it ever been rigorously challenged. Many free Blacks and escaped slaves now became fearful of losing what few rights they now enjoyed.

The Dred Scott decision (which among other things overturned the Missouri Compromise and thus threw the whole question of whether new states should be admitted as slave or free into chaos) caused a furor in the North. And the racist *obiter dicta* of Taney and his colleagues brought the

OPPOSITE TOP: Supreme Court Chief Justice Roger B. Taney (1777-1864). His decision in the 1857 Dred Scott case was one cause of the Civil War.

OPPOSITE BOTTOM: Dred Scott's wife, Harriet.

LEFT: Louis Schultze's portrait of Dred Scott (1793?-1858). In an *obiter dictum* Justice Taney held that Scott (or any Black) could never hold citizen's rights.

BELOW: The decision in the Dred Scott case was met with fury in the North.

issue of slavery starkly to the forefront of the many grievances that had been steadily driving the North and South apart for half a century. Unfortunately for the still-young republic, the institution of slavery had been getting stronger as time went on, not weaker. The number of slaves in the country had increased nearly five-fold since the Revolutionary War. Any hopes of reversing this trend seemed to be dashed by the Dred Scott ruling, as were hopes that America was progressing toward better race relations with the free Black population. The issue of slavery was not going to go away; it appeared resistant to reason, sentiment, negotiation, and now law. What remained to be seen was whether it could remain resistant to shot and shell.

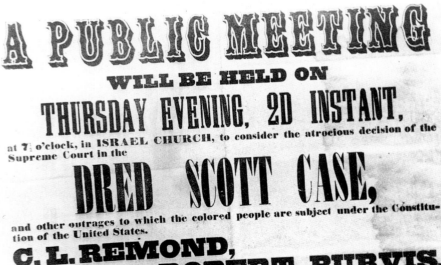

A PUBLIC MEETING
WILL BE HELD ON
THURSDAY EVENING, 2D INSTANT,
at 7½ o'clock, in ISRAEL CHURCH, to consider the atrocious decision of the Supreme Court in the
DRED SCOTT CASE,
and other outrages to which the colored people are subject under the Constitution of the United States.
C. L. REMOND,
ROBERT PURVIS,
and others will be speakers on the occasion. Mrs. MOTT, Mr. M'KIM and B. S. JONES of Ohio, have also accepted invitations to be present.
All persons are invited to attend. Admittance free.

Chapter Four

The American Civil War (1861-1865) was – and by most measures still is – the bloodiest conflict in the history of the republic. It was also one of the most definitive in the changes that it wrought throughout the land. But it may also be our nation's most misunderstood conflict in terms of its causes and results.

Though at the deepest level the war was about slavery, for a long time neither side was prepared to admit the fact. Lincoln insisted at first that the North was fighting solely to preserve the union. The Southern states claimed they were fighting for a concept of states rights, which opposed intrusion by the federal government into affairs that were properly the concern the states. Both positions had as much to do with political expediency as with truth.

To be sure, both sides did admit that at least one of the proximate causes of the war had to do with slavery, but not with its abolition. Rather, the dispute turned on whether new states being admitted to the Union would be slave or free. The issue here was largely political, since it affected the size of the Northern and Southern voting blocs in Congress.

Lincoln's Dilemma

Lincoln's avowed purpose was to save the Union first, and to check the advance of slavery into new land as a secondary consideration. At the same time, Lincoln's political dilemma was to keep the loyalty of the border states, which were ready to fight for the Union but wanted to keep their slaves, while appeasing the abolitionists, who wanted to strike a blow for freedom and emancipate the slaves. He also had to take into account the feelings of Northern anti-abolitionists, who were not prepared to fight and die for the cause of freeing the Black bondsmen. The contradictions inherent in this policy become vividly clear when we look at the way the North dealt with Blacks in its territory during the early years of the war.

When on April 12, 1861, the first shots in the war were fired at Ft. Sumter in Charleston Harbor, South Carolina,

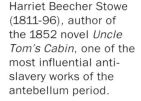

Harriet Beecher Stowe (1811-96), author of the 1852 novel *Uncle Tom's Cabin*, one of the most influential anti-slavery works of the antebellum period.

Civil War and Reconstruction, 1861-1877

ABOVE: J. S. Leary, a confederate of John Brown in his 1859 raid on Harper's Ferry.

LEFT: John Brown is led off to his place of execution. Brown (1800-59), a fanatic abolitionist, attacked the federal arsenal at Harper's Ferry, VA, as a prelude to what he hoped would become a general uprising of Southern slaves. He was caught and hanged, but many abolitionists saw him as a martyr.

ABOVE: John Copeland was another of John Brown's raiders. Like Brown, he was hanged.

RIGHT: In April 1861 South Carolina opened fire on federal Fort Sumter in Charleston Harbor. Lincoln still hoped that peace could be restored, but it was a vain hope. The Civil War had begun.

Northern Whites and Blacks answered the call to arms. Frederick Douglass urged African-Americans to join the Union armed forces, and a Black doctor from Battle Creek, Michigan, offered to raise a Black regiment of between 5,000 and 10,000 men. But Lincoln rejected all enlistment by African-Americans. The North certainly could have used their help in battle, but Lincoln judged that the political consequences of offending the border states and the anti-abolitionist groups in the North would simply be too great.

His policy toward newly-escaped Blacks was similarly deformed by political considerations. When the war began, African-American slaves flocked to Union lines seeking freedom. Some Union generals proclaimed they were free. But Lincoln initially took the position that the slaves should be returned to their masters. Not only was he worried about what the border states might think, his policy of preserving the Union at all costs meant that he had to behave as though the Union still existed in just the same form as it had before hostilities began. But if the Confederate states were legally still part of the Union, they were also still under the jurisdiction of the Constitution, and the Constitution

recognized slavery. Thus Lincoln argued that even if he felt sympathy for the escapees, he was bound by law to return them to their rightful owners. Lincoln clung to these increasingly threadbare lines of reasoning until 1862.

Meanwhile, the status of Blacks in the Union Army was still hazy. Slaves were barred from enlistment, and even free Blacks were not really welcomed. Yet escaped slaves were still flocking to Union lines. In fact, African-Americans were making a collective statement about their status in this country. Many slaves reasoned that Southerners couldn't keep an eye on both the Yankee army *and* the slaves. With a huge crack developing in the wall of White supremacy, the African slave was determined to slip through before it had time to repair itself. The only question left was what the North's response would be. The answer came in 1862.

Since slaves were *property* valuable to the enemy, the North found a way to legally accept the slaves. They were declared *contraband*, and this was somehow taken as a justification for letting them join the Union Army. But the designation left the central question unanswered, since Black men and women were now allowed to join the Union armed forces under the label of "valuable war material," not people.

Historians have argued about why Lincoln never called upon the slaves to rise in rebellion against their masters in the South. The reason once again was political, but it was more than just a sop to the border states and anti–abolitionists in the North. The fact is that, even though the North was losing the war in the early stages, *most* Northern Whites would never have countenanced calling on slaves to rise in revolt against Whites, even Confederates. Nor is it clear that Lincoln himself felt differently.

Many slaves escaping into Union territory were herded into what were called "contraband camps," but the North was unable to provide adequate food and shelter for the growing num-

ABOVE: A slave pen in Alexandria, VA. Even though both sides at first refused to admit it, the Civil War was, at the deepest level, fought over slavery.

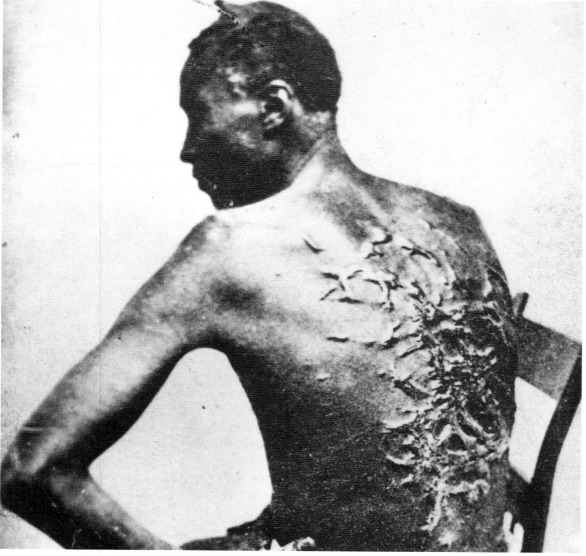

LEFT: The horribly scarred back of a slave in Louisiana who had been beaten by his owner.

A prayer meeting of a "contraband camp." The term "contraband" was used by Union forces early in the war to describe Blacks who had fled from slavery to Northern lines. By implying that they were captured enemy war material, the term avoided defining their citizenship status.

bers, and the escaped slaves there often suffered worse privation than they had under slavery. It was estimated that as many as one in four slaves in some camps died for lack of proper provisions. One response to this situation was that some men in the government proposed giving escaped slaves two acres each of abandoned captured Confederate land. This way the ex-slaves would be able to grow their own food and not be a drain on Union supplies, and they might even be able to produce a surplus which the Union could use in the war effort. Unfortunately, the plan never got off the ground. Squabbling between the Treasury Department and the Army resulted in only a few ex-slaves getting land, and much of the land captured by the Army wound up in the hands of Northern capitalists.

Even before the war there had been race riots in the North directed at African-Americans, most based on anti-abolitionist sentiment and fear of job competition. The situation did not change because of the war. In 1863 one of the worst race riots of the century occurred in New York City. Because White workers would not allow Blacks to join their unions, plant owners often used Black workers as strike-breakers when White workers struck for more money. That was the situation during the strike by New York dock workers in the summer of 1863. Of equal or greater concern to New York working men was growing resentment about being drafted into the Army, which they thought unfairly affected them and which, in any case, could result in introducing more Blacks into the competitive labor market. Added to this was the fact the war was going badly for the North on the battlefield. The result of these emotions and fears was a full-scale race riot. Blacks were attacked as they walked the streets. Stores and homes of Black people were also attacked, and an orphanage catering to Black children was burned to the

ABOVE: Whether any "contraband" should be admitted into the Union army was not at first clear. Many ex-slaves were given civilian jobs supporting the Federal forces.

LEFT: A family of escaped slaves comes to the Union lines.

ground. Scores of African-Americans were killed, some hanged from utility poles. The incident illustrated the vicious circle that was enveloping people of African descent in the North.

The Emancipation Proclamation, 1862-63

The Emancipation Proclamation was issued in September 1862. Lincoln had waited for a Union military victory (Shiloh) before issuing the controversial order. Superficially, the proclamation seemed at long last to acknowledge that the abolition of slavery really was one of the North's war aims, but in fact this famous declaration did less than it seemed to do.

The most memorable words in the order were, "all slaves held in areas in rebellion against the Union are free." But what did this really amount to? Lincoln had "freed" the slaves in the Confederacy, where his authority was not recognized. Moreover, by speaking of "areas in rebellion," he had not included the five slave-holding border states. Nor did his order apply to captured Southern lands already under Union control. What, then was the pur-

pose of issuing this proclamation that freed practically nobody?

Abraham Lincoln's primary goal in the war was to reunite the Union, and he had already noted that to do this he would consider freeing some, all, or none of the slaves. Given this set of priorities, it is possible that Lincoln may in some degree have thought of the Emancipation Proclamation as a sort of bargaining chip. He had purposely left a three months interval between the issuance of the document and the time it became law. Was he hoping to persuade the Southerners to lay down their arms and cease hostilities by implying that if they did so before the proclamation took effect they could resume their former status in the Union and keep their slaves? Would Lincoln in such a case have been prepared to withdraw the proclamation?

To be sure, the chances of the South's accepting such an offer at the end of 1862 were virtually nil, but the proclamation could have other useful political side-effects. By 1863 America was one of only three nations in the Western Hemisphere still to recognize slavery. (The other two countries were

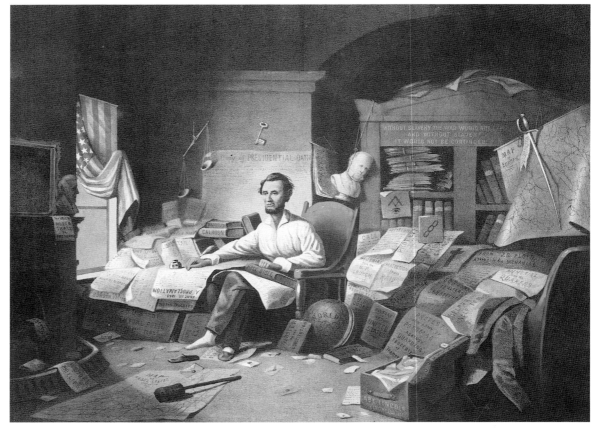

RIGHT: Abraham Lincoln writing the draft of the 1862 Emancipation Proclamation, as an artist imagined the scene. Although an important statement of Union war aims, the Proclamation in fact freed very few slaves.

Cuba and Brazil.) Europe had been pressing America to abolish the slave trade and the institution itself. Yet the Union blockade of all Southern ports had nearly brought France and England into the war on the side of the Confederacy, for they were outraged at being prevented by Union warships from buying Southern cotton. As long as Europe could argue that the issue between North and South was merely one of contested sovereignty, reasons could be found for favoring the South. But now that it appeared that the North was fighting to end slavery, European public opinion would make it impossible for any European government even to consider giving diplomatic recognition to the South or to protest too strongly against the blockade.

The proclamation did not, nor was it designed to, totally abolish slavery. Indeed, Lincoln's expressed personal views had always favored "gradual" emancipation, with voting rights at first limited to "intelligent" African-Americans. He had even toyed at one time with the idea of buying the state of Texas and setting this aside for the settlement of freedmen.

The Confederate Dilemma

Slavery caused wartime problems for the South as well as the North. Fear of slave revolts interfered with the working of conscription in the Confederacy, since some young men were always needed on the homefront to man the slave patrols: some states actually increased their slave patrols during the war. On the other hand, the South probably could not have fought the war without slave labor. It was the slaves who planted and harvested the crops, who continued to work the mines, docks and factories, who performed, in short, all the essential labor-intensive tasks that freed White men to fight.

The slaves in the South during this time were privy to the news of the war, but their response, in terms of action taken, was mixed. Almost none rebelled, some ran away to search for freedom behind the advancing Union lines, but most never left their plantations. Yet even here, the relationship between master and slave underwent some changes. Work slowdowns, increases in recalcitrant behavior, and increased reports of insubordination appeared to grow more common. Some slaves re-

OPPOSITE: Two views of ex-slaves working on a Southern plantation confiscated by Union troops. The ex-slaves are now paid wages — $.25 a day.

BELOW: South Carolina ex-slaves, freed by Union forces, drying cotton.

RIGHT TOP: Contraband Jackson in clothes he wore when a servant in the Confederate Army.

RIGHT BOTTOM: The same Jackson as a drummer in the Union Army.

fused to be punished, and some even began to demand wages for their labor. All this adversely affected production at a time when the South was already suffering severe economic distress as a result of the blockade.

Unlike the Union forces, the Confederate Army had enlisted Blacks from the start of the war: indeed, because of the manpower shortage, the Confederate government actually impressed slaves into military service. But the South could never get as many as it needed. Slave owners resisted the "slave draft" because they felt they were not paid a fair price by the Confederate authorities, and the slaves resisted military service. Once in the Confederate armed forces, the slaves filled non-combat roles such as cooks, laborers, teamsters, ambulance drivers, and, of course, personal body servants.

Near the war's end, there was some talk in the Confederacy of arming slaves, but this idea was quickly abandoned. Not only would such an action have exposed the South to the possibility of rebellion, it would have raised unanswerable questions about the status of Black veterans. Therein lay the essence of the South's dilemma. Though desperate for manpower, the South was a society based on White superiority and Black inferiority. If the South could only win the war with Black help, both the claim to White superiority and the basis of Southern society would be destroyed. This the South could not face. Thus the bigotry of race put the Confederacy in a quandary of color and helped to assure its defeat.

Blacks in Union Forces

It is estimated that by the war's end 186,000 African-Americans had joined the Union armed forces. Black soldiers were usually segregated into all-Black units commanded by White officers, and at first, many White officers resented commanding Black troops. But after African-Americans proved themselves in battle, most such resentment disappeared. Still, soldiers of African descent tended to get less pay than

ABOVE: By 1863 the African-American presence in the Union forces was already considerable. Here, some men of the 107th Infantry.

White soldiers of the same rank. White corporals average $16.50 per month, blacks only $10.

Probably most Blacks in Union forces performed non-combat duties, the many who did fight distinguished themselves in battles such as those at Fort Wagner and Port Hudson. In addition, ex-slaves such as Harriet Tubman proved invaluable as Union spies: it was fairly easy for them to slip behind Confederate lines, where they could pass for lost slaves looking for their masters.

Black sailors made up one-fourth of the men in the Union Navy, 29,000 of 118,000. Not all were stewards and cooks, for many proved valuable as pilots for Union vessels in Southern waters (just as they had done in the previous century in service during the Revolutionary War).

African-American casualties in the Union fighting forces were four times as high as those of Whites, some 38,000,

LEFT: A Black infantry corporal poses for his portrait. The revolver is probably a studio prop, since it is a non-regulation Model 1849 Colt.

ABOVE: An 1865 photo of the 26th Colored Infantry on parade at Camp William Penn in Pennsylvania.

NEAR RIGHT: Navyman John H. Lawson won the Medal of Honor for his part in the Battle of Mobile Bay in 1864.

FAR RIGHT: Robert Smalls (1839-1925) stole a Rebel ship and delivered it to the Union. He later served in the U.S. House of Representatives.

or one in five, were killed. The high casualty rate had several causes. Confederates treated many captured African-Americans as rebellious slaves. Sometimes, even when Black troops surrendered, they were massacred, as was the case at Ft. Pillow. This fort, largely defended by Black troops, was overrun by Rebel forces commanded by Gen. Nathan Bedford Forrest. When the fort surrendered, Confederate troops killed not only most of the Black soldiers but also many Black women and children. (Gen. Forrest later helped found the Ku Klux Klan.) Other causes of casualties in the Union Army were the facts that Black soldiers tended to be sent into battle with the least preparation, and the poorest equipment and that they often got the poorest medical attention when wounded.

LEFT: Christian A. Fleetwood of the 4th Colored Infantry won the Medal of Honor for gallantry during the capture of Rebel Fort Harrison in 1864.

BELOW: Contrabands on board the U.S.S. *Vermont*.

RIGHT: Holt Collier, one of many Blacks who fought for the South during the Civil War.

BELOW: C.S.A. General Stonewall Jackson's personal cook.

The Union Wins the War

On April 9, 1865, Confederate General Robert E. Lee surrendered to Union General Ulysses S. Grant at Appomattox Court House, Virginia, and for all practical purposes the long agony of the Civil War was over. It had been a gruesome business by any standard. Of all the wars America has ever fought, only World War II produced a larger number of casualties. But if we think of those casualties in relation to total populations, even World War II pales in comparison. Casualties in the Civil War amounted to 2.5 percent of the population of the U.S. in 1860. If the same percentage had been applied to the U.S. population in 1940, World War II would have produced 3.3 million American casualties – more than triple the actual figure. As a percentage of today's population, the Civil War's casualty rate would be the equivalent of about 6.2 million dead and wounded. That was the real magnitude of the disaster, and it left physical and psychological scars on North and South alike.

Though the North had lost many more men in the war than did the South, it suffered relatively little economic damage: indeed, the Union's $4 billion in direct wartime expenditures had proven a boon to Northern industry and had generated many handsome profits. Yet there remained in the North much rancor against the South, which was wholly blamed for starting the war, and this vindictiveness would continue to affect the North's policies toward the South for most of the postwar decade. Certainly the North's bitterness was in no way softened when, on April 14, just five days after Lee's surrender at Appomattox, a Southern fanatic named John Wilkes Booth assassinated President Abraham Lincoln while he was attending the theater in Washington, D.C.

The war had wrecked the South. In addition to the ruination visited on such cities as Atlanta, Charleston, Richmond, Mobile, and Vicksburg, large swaths of the countryside had been devastated, as had many roads, bridges, and rail lines. The South's bank reserves had been wiped out, its

Liberated slaves in Richmond, VA; the Confederate capital, photographed shortly after the Union took the city in 1865.

credit system was a shambles, the value of its plantation land had been cut by over 50 percent, and its estimated $2.5 billion investment in the institution of slavery had evaporated.

At the war's end most Southern slave-owners bowed to the inevitable and acknowledged their slaves' freedom without waiting until they were forced to do so by federal laws and Union troops. Continued resistance would, at this point, have been self-defeating. The North, as early as February 1865, had proposed a new amendment to the Constitution – the Thirteenth – outlawing slavery, and it was clear to everyone that, even under the most lenient imaginable postwar reconstruction plan, ratification of this amendment would be one of the conditions that any defeated Southern state would have to meet in order to free itself from martial rule and be re-admitted to the Union. In fact, by December 1865 enough Southern states had ratified the Thirteenth Amendment to make it the law of the land.

The readiness of Southern slave owners to accept the legal end of slavery was accelerated by sheer economic necessity. All of the South was now poor, and some of it was starving. Black labor was needed as never before, now not for profit but simply for survival. Ex-slave-owners were desperate to persuade as many Black freedmen as possible to stay where they were, working the land for wages or for a share of the crop.

Some freedmen would have none of this and moved away, but many stayed, feeling that times were, at least for the moment, too desperate to give them much choice. Whatever they chose to do, all freedmen had to face bewildering changes, not only in their formal relations with Whites but in such small but basic matters as having their marriages consecrated and recognized by law or adopting legal surnames. Regarding names, some simply took the names of their former masters, while others, finding this distasteful, chose the names of famous Americans, such as Washington, Jefferson, or Jackson.

Historians have often speculated

ABOVE: Andrew Johnson, Lincoln's successor, wanted to treat the conquered South with such lenience that Southern Whites could have denied ex-slaves even the most basic civil rights.

RIGHT: Optimists in the North hailed the end of slavery as the ultimate victory over oppression, but it was only a battle won in a long struggle still to be fought.

were seen as too lenient by many, both in and out of the Congress. The two years following the war are generally called the period of Presidential Reconstruction. It would be overshadowed, and its policies largely undone, in the ten-year period (1867-77) when Congress exercised control over the conquered South.

Since Lincoln never viewed the South as having left the Union, it is not surprising that his Reconstruction plan was rather mild, all things considered. He proposed that any Southern state could begin sending representatives back to Congress as soon as one-tenth of the numbers of voters who had voted in the 1860 election swore a loyalty oath to the Union. Those who took the loyalty oath would also be granted amnesty. This may have been all very well for healing the wounds caused by the war, but notably absent were any provision for voting, civil rights, or reparations for the ex-slaves. Whatever the merits of the plan, Lincoln's assassination prevented it from ever being put into effect.

Andrew Johnson had come to the vice-presidency through the United States Senate, but he was disliked by many in the Congress, and not least because he had once owned slaves. Johnson's plan to re-integrate the

about why the newly-freed slaves committed so few acts of violence or revenge against their former masters. Some have suggested that two centuries of bondage had instilled in the slaves a spirit of docility that they could not immediately shake off. A more likely explanation has to do with their essential humanity, their sense that the wrongs that had been done them would never be set right by committing fresh wrongs. But probably most to the point was simply that their attention was now focused not on the past but on their hopes for the future. Unfortunately, those hopes were to meet with many disappointments.

Presidential Reconstruction, 1865-1867

During the war Lincoln had drawn up a plan to re-integrate the South into the Union, but before he could implement the program he was assassinated. His place was taken by the Vice-President, Andrew Johnson, whose plan was similar to Lincoln's. But both these plans

South into the Union varied little from that of his predecessor. In fact, Johnson's three-point program incorporated two of Lincoln's. The third, different, point was temporary denial of the vote to Southerners who had property valued at more than $20,000. To understand Johnson's thinking, one must know something of his background.

Johnson was born in Tennessee into the poor White class, and even as a child he had evinced a hatred of rich planters. He also disliked Blacks, though after becoming successful he owned slaves. While serving in the U.S. Senate he had even advocated annexing Cuba as a slave state so that the institution could expand. As President, Johnson thus saw himself as a champion of the "little (White) Southern man" at the expense of the rich planters, and though he supported abolition in theory, it may be doubted if he felt very strongly about the matter.

Johnson made his offer to the South in May 1865, when Congress was still in recess. Southern voters could elect members to a constitutional convention in each state. These conventions were to abolish slavery, rescind the state's secession ordinance, adopt the Thirteenth Amendment, repudiate the state's war debt, and arrange for the election of a new state government. Significantly, the states themselves could determine who could vote in these elections, which virtually guaranteed the exclusion of Blacks. Once all this had been done, the states could be readmitted to the Union.

Southern Whites of course took such a lenient Reconstruction policy as a signal that they could return to business as usual. By the end of 1865 all the Southern states but Texas had met Johnson's terms and were busily electing former Confederate officials to local and Congressional posts. Even former Confederate Vice President Alexander Stephens was elected to the U.S. Senate from his home state of Georgia.

Now that slavery was officially over, the old slave laws were invalid, but Southerners simply substituted the word "Black" for "Slave" and came up

A U.S. officer tries to head off racial violence in front of a Freedmen's Bureau office in the postwar South.

with the "Black Codes". These were laws and measures designed to reduce the freedman to positions of second- or third-class citizenship. The freedmen weren't slaves any longer, but they still couldn't vote or hold office. They still had no money or land, and virtually no protection under the law.

Radical Reconstruction Policy, 1867-1877

Many in the North, and even some Southerners, were surprised and shocked by what they were seeing. After four years of bloody conflict, hundreds of thousands of lives lost, and millions of dollars in property loss, the South was, in their view, getting off far too easily for the pain and suffering it had caused, and the Union was being cheated of some of its most basic war aims. Among the most vehement opponents of the Lincoln-Johnson Reconstruction policy were members of the so-called "radical" wing of the Republican Party in Congress, who bitterly resented seeing ex-Confederate officials being sent back to the House and Senate. The Republicans had enjoyed the prestige of being labeled the party of the Union during the war, yet now they were threatened with losing their positions of power to a coalition of Southern Democrats and their counterparts in the North.

Northern industrialists were also displeased with the direction of Presidential Reconstruction. The South was not only going to back to its old social ways, it seemed to stand a chance of duplicating the economy of the antebellum period. Northern industry, flush with success and profits from the war, had no desire to face competition from a revived South but did have a strong interest in being able to make use of the cheap labor that had now become available in the ex-Confederate states.

But political and economic self-interest were by no means the only things that informed Northerners' attitudes towards Reconstruction. There was a deep and very widespread feeling that the South deserved to be punished, and though there was no real consensus about what form the punishment should take, there was a general sense that the Presidential Reconstruction plans fell short of what was wanted.

Inevitably, it was the Republican radicals in Congress who spearheaded the attack on the Johnson plan, but they had no lack of public support, as would be demonstrated by their winning a two-thirds majority in each

A village erected for freedmen in Arlington, VA, at the war's end.

house in the Congressional elections of 1866. Their first moves were to gain passage (over Johnson's vetos) of The New Freedmen's Bureau Bill (February 1866) and The Civil Rights Act (April 1866), both aimed at protecting freedmen from the effects of the "Black Codes." To make sure that this legislation would be safe from challenge on constitutional grounds, the radicals proposed the Fourteenth Amendment, which spelled out the essense of the protections they sought.

But these were merely first steps. The radicals' real blow was struck in March 1867 with the passage (also over Johnson's veto) of the First Reconstruction Act. In effect, this act declared that the governments of all the Southern states that had been created under the Johnson plan were, with the single exception of Tennessee, illegal. New state constitutional conventions were to be assembled, this time based on "universal" manhood suffrage, though in fact most prominent ex-Confederates were excluded from either voting or holding high office. Ratification of the Fourteenth Amendment was to be a prerequisite to re-admission but not a guarantee of it, for Congress reserved the right to review all proposed new systems of state government and

to reject any it did not like. Meantime, the South was to be carved up into five military districts subject to martial law, with the commanding general of each district being the final arbiter of who could and could not vote.

This Congressional Reconstruction plan was certainly harsh in concept, but it was far harsher in application, because in some areas it soon became mired in corruption and administrative bungling. It caused enough unnecessary and unfair hardship in the South that in the end it proved self-defeating, hardening Southern resentment and resistance while steadily losing support in the North. Yet for African-Americans it accomplished much – at least in the short term.

The Transition to Freedom

For newly-liberated slaves, the change of status from sub-human chattel to full citizenship came so abruptly (about 12 months) that it produced much disorientation and psychological stress. Suddenly, for example, the master was no longer head of the freedman's household; now the Black man of the house had to assume the role of protector and provider – no easy task for people without money, and barely with shelter, cast adrift in a land devas-

Angry Southern Whites murder a Black man in one of the many race riots that plagued the Reconstructed South.

81

become African-Americans, and for most, "home" was now here, not there. At least in theory, they had gained their freedom, but the struggle to secure happiness and dignity still law ahead. The overwhelming majority elected to fight that battle here.

Role of the Black Churches

A few organizations were in place to help the freedmen make the difficult transition to freedom, and of these, the Black Christian churches may have been the most important. The Black churches had come into being largely as a result of the pervasive racism of White churches, and they were by far

ABOVE: The Democrats had regained control of Southern politics by the early 1870s. As Republicans were voted out of state offices, Reconstruction waned.

TOP RIGHT: African-American Methodist Episcopal Church founder Richard Allen (1760-1831).

BOTTOM RIGHT: Thomas Paul (1773-1831), the first pastor of the African Baptist Church.

tated by war. Families that slavery had torn apart had painfully to try to reassemble themselves (which was often impossible) and make a new beginning. Ex-slave men and women had to adjust to changing domestic and social roles within the family structure. And all freedmen had to confront anew the question of their true ethnic identity. In the past, amid the horrors and degradation of slavery, many had clung to their "African-ness," had associated all thoughts of freedom, happiness, and dignity with "home," with Africa. But Africa had grown to seem increasingly far away, not only in distance and accessibility but in time and memory. For good or ill, the ex-slaves had the most powerful of Black institutions. (Indeed, they are still one of the few categories of institutions that African-Americans control politically and economically.) During and after Reconstruction the Black churches served not only the spiritual aspirations of the Black community but also their educational, political, economic, and even entertainment needs. Black churches served as travelers' aid societies, bases for political action, and sources of education. Many Black churches founded elementary, high schools and colleges during the Reconstruction.

The Freedmen's Bureau, 1865-1872

The federally-sponsored Freedmen's Bureau was another institution that tried to care for the needs of newly-freed slaves. One of its major duties was to supervise the redistribution of land from Southern plantations to former slaves and poor Whites. But the bureau had a difficult time fulfilling its mandate because of its many enemies both in the North and the South. A good many Northerners saw the bureau as a waste of time and money, arguing that now that slavery was over, there was no need to give any preferred treatment to the freedmen. And almost all Southerners looked upon the bureau as another humiliating intrusion by the federal government into the internal affairs of the Southern states. The idea of their tax money going to aid what had only a short time earlier been their property was especially galling.

Yet even though the Freedmen's Bureau significantly helped only a small percentage of the freedmen, it did leave a lasting legacy, by far its most significant and lasting contribution being in the field of education. Many Northern White women came south to staff and run elementary and secondary schools for those many ex-slaves who thirsted after knowledge. Such freedmen especially wanted to learn to read and write, as these skills were seen as the keys to a better life. Moreover, an impressive number of Black colleges and universities were founded with the help of the Freedmen's

LEFT: P.B.S. Pinchback (1837-1921), the first Black governor of a state (Louisiana).

BELOW: African-Americans who served in the U.S. Senate during Reconstruction.

ABOVE: In the 44th Congress (1875-77), the South Carolina delegation included J. H. Rainey, the first African-American U.S. Representative, and Robert Smalls, a war hero. Both served five terms in Congress.

RIGHT: Blanche Kelso Bruce (1841-98) of Mississippi was the first African-American to serve a full term in the U.S. Senate (1875-81).

men's Bureau, among the most notable being Fisk University, Howard University, and Atlanta University.

Black Politics and Politicians, 1867-1877

As a result of the First Reconstruction Act of 1867 and of its constitutional underpinning in the Fourteenth Amendment (ratified in July 1868), African-Americans were for the first time fully enfranchised. Now, armed with the vote, freedmen and free Blacks alike wanted to make sure that those elected to draw up the new state constitutions had their interests at heart.

Politically, this period of the Reconstruction will probably never be equaled again, at least at the state level. Because some Southern Whites had lost the vote as a punishment for their involvement in the war, there were Black voting majorities in five Southern states, and Blacks were thus in a position to decide the election of the state legislature, governor, senators, etc. In terms of performance, Black politicians of this period ran the gamut, from poor to excellent, but in this they were no different from their White counterparts, and their task was both more daunting and more urgent. The level of some of the gains made by Blacks have only recently been duplicated. During Reconstruction the nation had its first and only Black governor until L. Douglas Wilder was elected governor of Virginia in 1989. (Governor Wilder is the nation's second Black governor but he is the nation's first *elected* Black governor.) The nation's first African-American governor was Pinckney Benton Stewart Pinchback of Louisiana. He was elected as lieutenant governor but assumed the governorship when the White governor was impeached.

During Black Reconstruction African-Americans at various times and places occupied nearly every kind of elected office, from state governor down to town council. Alonzo Ransier was elected lieutenant governor of South Carolina in 1870. South Carolina also saw Robert Elliott and Samuel Lee elected speakers of the state's House of

School teachers sent by the Freedmen's Bureau to instruct poor Southern Black and White children after the war.

Representatives. The nation also saw its first Blacks elected to the United States Senate: Hiram Revels and Blanche Bruce were both elected from the state of Mississippi. (After Reconstruction there would be no other African-Americans elected to the Senate until 1966, when Edward Brooke of Massachusetts won the seat.) The House of Representatives welcomed 20 African-Americans during the era. Robert Smalls and J. H. Rainey, both of South Carolina, served the longest, at five terms each. All across the former Confederacy, African-Americans as a group were voting and serving in office for the first time in the history of the republic. And, it should be noted, all of these officials were members of the Republican Party. (History was made on two levels in 1992 with the election of Carol Moseley-

Braun of Illinois: not only was she the first African-American woman to serve in the Senate, she was also the first Black *Democratic* Senator ever elected.)

When Blacks were finally elected to office they set about dealing with some of the pressing problems facing not only African-Americans but many Whites as well. One such problem was that of literacy. The idea of free public education had never seriously been pursued in most Southern states until the Black-dominated legislatures of the Reconstruction era took up the cause. In some states African-Americans even assumed the position of state director of public education. Though it was of benefit to Blacks, this determined assault on illiteracy was also plainly a matter of the common good, for a great many Southern Whites had also been too poor to be able to afford the cost of even a rudimentary education.

With Blacks now in office, the first laws that were eliminated were all those

supporting racial segregation. The state constitutions drawn up during this era were some of the most liberal and complete documents the country had ever seen. In some respects they surpassed those of most Northern states in their concern for social issues. It was as if the South were getting a new lease on government, now that the former planter class had ceased wielding such a disproportionate amount of power. In general, the Reconstruction-era state constitutions were so well drawn that they remained almost unchanged when Southern Whites began to regain power. What was changed, unfortunately, were the laws relating to segregation.

Why Black Reconstruction Failed

The same partisan political forces that helped start Black Reconstruction were also instrumental in bringing about its demise. The struggle between Democrats and Republicans for control of the national government in time became so intense that both parties lost sight of the interests of the freedman —

or rather, the fate of the freedman became ever less a matter of principle and ever more a subject of compromise in the endless Washingtonian game of partisan maneuver.

The harsh truth was that the cause of the freedman was losing its hold over the imagination of Northern liberal Republicans, the only sector of the White electorate on which Blacks had ever been able to count during the post-Civil War years. The vengeful anti-Southern sentiments that had stirred so many Republicans immediately after the war were fading, and at the same time, many Republican moderates were becoming increasingly disgusted by the mismanagement and corruption that the radical Republicans in Congress had allowed to creep into aspects of their administration of the Reconstruction process. Perhaps more basically, the attention of the Northern electorate as a whole was beginning to wander off to other, more self-interested concerns — the lure of westward expansion, the fulminating growth of big industry (especially oil, steel and railroads) and big

banking, the rise of organized labor, new urban and rural problems, and much else. Thus, as the Republican electorate began to lose its commitment to Reconstruction, to Black voting and civil rights, so did Republican politicians.

How Black Reconstruction Ended

Though the date 1877 is often given for the end of Reconstruction, that is not completely accurate. In some cases the end came sooner: for example, the end of the Freedmen's Bureau came in 1872. In other instances, the gains of Reconstruction lasted beyond 1877, since all Blacks did not suddenly lose the right to vote in that year. Yet undeniably, the date does mark a symbolic turning point, both in the history of American politics and in the fate of African-Americans.

The presidential election of 1876 turned into a very close and corrupt race between Rutherford B. Hayes (Republican) and Samuel Tilden (Democrat). The final popular vote showed Tilden the winner, with 4,284,000 votes

A reunion of the Yale class of 1874. Marked "10" (row 2, fourth from right) is Edward A. Bouchet, the first African-American to be given a degree from a White university. He was Phi Beta Kappa and went on to receive his Ph.D. from Yale in 1876.

87

ABOVE: A drawing based on a photograph taken in 1870 of three Ku Klux Klansmen in the disguises they were wearing when captured by the police.

(52 percent) to Hayes's 4,036,000 votes (48 percent). But the vote in the Electoral College was much closer. In a "backroom" deal, Hayes courted the electoral votes of a number of Southern states, in return promising that if he were elected he would withdraw all remaining federal troops from the South and would essentially adopt a hands-off policy regarding the internal affairs of the Southern states. Enough Southern states agreed to this deal to give Hayes the presidency: 185 electoral votes to Tilden's 184. The following year, Hayes took office and, true to his word, withdrew the last of the Federal troops. The way was now open for the White South to begin its attack on the newly-won rights of the freedmen in earnest.

How did the White South go about the business of putting the African-American back into "his place"? Any and all means were used, from threats to violence to outright murder. It was during this era that the Ku Klux Klan was formed — by former Confederate

RIGHT: Accused of the rape of a White woman, Albert Martin is dragged by a White mob from the jail in Port Huron, MI, in 1889 and murdered.

General Nathan Bedford Forest in 1868. Blacks and sympathetic Whites were attacked and threatened. African-Americans were discouraged from seeking elected office and even from trying to vote. Southerners dusted off the old Slave Codes and changed the name to "Jim Crow" laws. The basis of the new laws was complete and perpetuated separation of the races, with special emphasis on keeping Black men away from White women.

One of the biggest problems in writing Jim Crow laws was trying to define what was meant by the terms "Negro" or "Black". In the end, the criterion came down to deciding how much "Black blood" (what was known as the "Black quantum") a person had. Thus various states defined a "Negro" as someone having ½, ¼, ⅛, 1⁄16, or even one or two drops of Black blood.

In order to justify these vicious policies, White Southerners launched a propaganda attack on the entire history of Black Reconstruction, painting its shortcomings in the most luridly negative colors possible and falsifying facts where necessary. The myth-makers aimed their venom at three groups: Northern Whites, Southern Whites, and Blacks:

1. *Northern Whites.* During Reconstruction a number of White Northerners came South to work in the Reconstruction governments, which were open to all, thanks to the power and influence of the newly-freed Black vote. While some probably came South mainly to see if they could line their pockets, many others were liberal idealists who hoped to help build a truly democratic society. But the only image of the White Northerners that Southerners wanted the world to see was of a group of scoundrels interested in nothing more than stealing as much money as they could and brutally oppressing and humiliating Southern Whites. The derogatory name given such people was "carpetbaggers," deriving from the fact that much of their luggage was made of the same material used in carpets and rugs. In short, a large and diverse group of

people was defined solely in terms of its worst elements — a classic propaganda tactic.

2. *Southern Whites.* Southerners who supported Reconstruction were probably hated more even than the Yankee carpetbaggers. Such individuals came to be called "scalawags" and were uniformly vilified as corrupt thieves aiding and abetting the rape of the South by the vengeful North. There were not, in fact, a great many Southern pro-Reconstructionists, but, since treachery is always a despised crime, the myth-makers found it convenient to exaggerate the scalawags' numbers and activities grossly.

3. *Blacks.* The freedmen were, of course, the most important target of all, but the Southern propagandists chose to attack them somewhat more obliquely. The keynote of the attack was to stress the innate stupidity and gullibility of Blacks and to shed crocodile tears over the ruthless way in which they had been manipulated by evil carpetbaggers and scalawags. The clear implication was that since Blacks were congenitally inferior, they were

Two stereotypes that Southern propaganda deliberately fostered: the gullible freedman and the unscrupulous carpetbagger.

incapable of self-government. The best thing that could happen to them would be for them to be governed by competent people who genuinely understood them and their proper place in society. And who could possibly understand such things better than Southern Whites? Q.E.D.

Put so badly, the arguments of the Southern myth-makers sound absurd, yet they were horribly effective. Nearly all Southern Whites believed them, and so did a good many Northern Whites. That there was some corruption in the Reconstruction process is undeniable, yet too few people then – and even now – paused to put the matter into perspective. Modern scholars have estimated, for example, that during roughly the same time that Black Reconstruction was flourishing in the South, "Boss" William Tweed's Tammany Hall ring stole more money from New York City alone than was ever stolen from all the Reconstruction governments combined. To dwell on Reconstruction's (probably inevitable) shortcomings, while ignoring its obvious accomplishments, was, and is, simply folly. Yet that is what the Southern propagandists sought to make people do, and they succeeded beyond all reason.

An 1867 lithograph from *Frank Leslie's Illustrated Newspaper* shows a jury composed of Blacks and Whites in the Reconstruction-era South.

The Court

The relentlessly conservative U.S. Supreme Court also played a role in the destruction of Black Reconstruction. It did this through a series of rulings that greatly weakened key laws designed to protect the rights of the newly-freed slave. Thus, in 1883, the Supreme Court effectively declared the Civil Rights Act of 1875 unconstitutional. (The Civil Rights Act of 1875 was in many respects identical to the Civil Rights Act of 1964.) It did so by delivering devastating reinterpretations of the Fourteenth and Fifteenth Amendments. A summary of these amendments is given below:

Fourteenth Amendment
All persons born or naturalized in the United States, and subject to the jurisdiction thereof, are citizens of the United States and of the State wherein they reside. No State shall make or enforce any law which shall abridge the privileges or immunities of citizens of the United States; nor shall any State deprive any person of life, liberty, or property, without due process of law; nor deny to any person within its jurisdiction the equal protection of the laws.
Fifteenth Amendment
The right of citizens of the United States to vote shall not be denied or abridged by the United States or by any State on account of race, color, or previous condition of servitude.

The Court took the position that the Fourteenth Amendment did not guarantee Black people freedom from racial discrimination. Rather, the court ruled that the amendment only prohibited *states* from discriminating, but not *individuals*! Therefore an individual, or company, or place of public accommodation, could freely discriminate on the basis of race.

In a case involving the Fifteenth Amendment the justices held that the amendment did not really guarantee the freedman the right to vote. All the amendment stated, according to the Court's view, was that an individual could not be *denied* the vote because of his race, color, or previous condition of

servitude. The Southern states quickly responded to this ruling by concocting any number of restrictions on voting rights based on other grounds: grandfather clauses, poll taxes, literacy tests, and so on. The South could now begin legally to remove African-Americans from voting lists and thus from public office.

Reconstruction: A Balance Sheet

The Reconstruction period was the most racially democratic time seen thus far in American political history. For the first time, African-Americans played an active, important part in the "body politic" and the political process. And this occurred in the South, for it had yet to happen so completely in the North, and, indeed, would have to wait well into the next century for anything comparable.

Superficially, it seemed that the Union victory in the Civil War had been a triumph for African-Americans. Slavery had been abolished and African-Americans who had been held as slaves were property no longer. But it was still a long way from being a "non-slave" to becoming a full citizen. Consider what the situation was 25 years after the Civil War ended:

1. By 1890 most Southern Whites had regained the vote.
2. Most Blacks had lost the vote due to the legal and illegal tactics of Southerners. Few Blacks were still voting and fewer still held office.

3. Since most African-Americans did not get land after emancipation, they had to go back to their former owners for their livelihood. Most freedmen became sharecroppers and tenant farmers.
4. Jim Crow laws had made the citizenship status of the freedman little better than it had been before the war.

Emancipation had brought an end to slavery, but it did not bring an end to racism or secure Black civil rights. Yet, the freedman remained guardedly optimistic. His assessment of the situation is embodied in a saying passed down from the era. It goes: "We ain't what we ought to be, we ain't what we going to be. But thank God we ain't what we used to be."

Two views of an open polling booth in a Southern town during Reconstruction. The gains made by Blacks during this 12-year period would not be equalled until the mid-twentieth century.

Chapter Five

As the turn of the century drew near, a postslave generation of African-Americans confronted a rising tide of racism and economic hardships little mitigated by emancipation and Reconstruction. The Black community was divided as to the best course of action: What tactics would ensure fulfillment of the hopes dashed in the postwar years? Frederick Douglass died in 1895, after half a century of leadership, and the men who moved into the forefront of the struggle for Black liberation, Booker T. Washington and W.E.B. Du Bois, were divided in their views. Simply put, Washington saw separation as the way to Black empowerment, while Du Bois focused on integration.

Booker T. Washington (1856-1915)

Booker Taliaferro Washington was born a slave in 1856 in Franklin County, Virginia. His mother was a cook and his father, a local White man. His childhood was typical for African-Americans of the period in that he never knew the exact date of his birth or his father's identity. He chose the surname "Washington" himself and became determined to get an education. Though his goal wasn't unusual, the fact that he succeeded was.

As he described it in his autobiography *Up From Slavery* (1901), Washington set out in 1872 for Hampton Institute in Hampton, Virginia, a school for African-Americans founded by former Union officer Samuel C. Armstrong. Since he lived nearly 200 miles from Hampton and had little money, he made the trip on foot and by hitchhiking, sleeping outdoors along the way. When he applied for admission to the school, the registrar gave him a rag and a bucket of water and told him to clean out one of the classrooms. He passed this unusual entrance exam.

Like most African-American college students of his day, Washington worked his way through school, mainly by performing manual labor for the Institute. During his senior year at Hampton, in order to help the incoming freshmen, he and a group of upper classmen volunteered to spend the winter months in tents, so the new students could share the school's only dormitory.

At Hampton, Washington was greatly influenced by General Samuel C. Armstrong. With many Whites of the period,

The great Booker T. Washington (sitting, left) with some members of the faculty at the Tuskegee Normal and Industrial Institute in Macon County, AL.

Old Problems, New Solutions, 1877-1954

Armstrong believed that Black students should get a vocational-technical education stressing manual labor and technical training rather than the liberal arts. Many of the school's construction, maintenance, and custodial duties were performed by the students, since money was scarce. At Hampton these tasks extended to growing crops and other food items. Implicit in the system was an emphasis on cleanliness, thrift, and the dignity of manual labor. This philosophy dominated the approach to Black education for decades, and Washington became its staunch advocate over the objections of many Black intellectuals. To this day, many historically Black colleges and universities carry the designations A&M (for Agricultural and Mechanical), A&T (Agriculture and Technology), and A&I (Agriculture and Industry.)

After graduation, in 1875, Washington taught school in West Virginia and spent a year at Wayland Seminary in Washington, D.C. He returned to Hampton as an instructor in 1879 and directed a night school for Black students who worked in local industries by day to pay for their education. In 1881 General Armstrong recommended him as director of a new school for African-Americans in Tuskegee, Alabama.

At first, the local White community was opposed to the idea of a Black college in its midst. But Washington assured the local opposition that the college would be an asset. He stressed the mutuality of interests between Blacks and Whites and pointed out that the school could train Black share-

ABOVE: One of Booker T. Washington's star teachers at Tuskegee was famous scientist George Washington Carver (1864-1943), shown here (center) with some pupils.

LEFT: At Tuskegee, agriculture students harrow a field.

ABOVE: Black inventor Jan Matzeliger (1852-1889) patented a shoe lasting machine that made Lynn, MA, "the shoe capital of the world."

ABOVE RIGHT: The shoemaking shop at Tuskegee.

BELOW: Lewis Howard Latimer (1848-1928), who became the chief draughtsman for both General Electric and Westinghouse, had made the patent drawings for Alexander Graham Bell's first telephone.

croppers to be more productive. Eventually, Washington won support, not only from his apprehensive local opposition but from powerful Northern philanthropists like Andrew Carnegie.

Washington opened the school with some 30 students whose first classes were held in an abandoned chicken coop donated by a local farmer. The curriculum was patterned after that of Hampton Institute and was designed to improve the economic condition of African-Americans without making them dissatisfied with the existing sociopolitical order. After 14 years of tireless effort as both educator and fundraiser, Washington had established Tuskegee Normal and Industrial Institute as a powerful influence on national thinking and the capital of Black America.

In 1895 Washington was chosen to deliver an address at the Cotton States Exposition in Atlanta. At this landmark meeting in the effective capital of the New South, he proposed a formula for race relations that allayed White fears of equal rights and turned many Blacks against him. His theme was that Blacks would best protect their constitutional rights through their own economic and moral progress and that the best approach to civil rights in the South was to let the issue alone: it would take care of itself.

After this address, often called the Atlanta Compromise speech, Washington's critics became more vocal. Many African-Americans questioned the degree of his influence and accused him of supporting segregation and discrimination. "In all things social" he said, "we separate as the fingers, yet [balling his hand into a fist] one as the hand in all things essential to mutual progress."

When the Supreme Court ruled the following year, in *Plessy v. Ferguson*, that "separate but equal" facilities for Blacks were constitutional, Washington's critics blamed him for upholding institutional segregation.

To implement his ideas, Washington started the National Negro Business League, still in existence, to give African-Americans a foothold in the world of commerce, and he set up many rural extension programs. He initiated a trade program to develop economic ties between West Africa and the United States before World War I, but it was interrupted by the hostilities. To the end of his life, in 1915, he preferred to work outside the political arena, even withdrawing himself from consideration for a Cabinet post in the McKinley administration in 1896.

In his work *Rebellion or Revolution?* (1968) Harold Cruse argued that the Nation of Islam (Black Muslims) and its

ABOVE: Author, editor and educator W. E. B. Du Bois (1868-1963).

LEFT: Graduates of Spelman Seminary in Atlanta in 1893. They would give religious and moral training in Black communities throughout Georgia.

leader Malcolm X (born Malcolm Little) were contemporary manifestations of Washington's ideas on Black nationalism. Cruse declared that Washington was not against civil rights but wanted to tone down the rhetoric in favor of the movement because of the danger to Blacks. He was outspoken in his denunciation of lynching and other forms of mob violence against African-Americans.

William Edward Burghardt Du Bois, 1868-1963

W. E. B. Du Bois, one of the most influential men of the twentieth century, was born in 1868 in Great Barrington, Massachusetts. His mother was Black and his father, mulatto, of mixed African, Dutch, and French ancestry. The couple was affluent by the standards of the day and encouraged the educational aspirations of their gifted son. Du Bois was graduated from Springfield (MA) High School at the top of his class. He was rejected in his first application to Harvard University and entered Fisk University, historically a Black liberal arts college, in Nashville, Tennessee, in the early 1880s. His formal education and full scholarship enabled him to enter as a sophomore rather than a freshman.

At Fisk, the young Du Bois experienced an all-Black environment for the first time. He became aware of the struggle that most African-Americans faced from day to day. He was influenced to devote his talents to ending racial oppression using education as his primary tool. Unlike Booker T. Washington, he believed that it was vital for Blacks to enhance their own aesthetic and cultural values even as they worked toward their eventual social emancipation.

In 1888 Du Bois entered Harvard on a full scholarship. There he earned a second bachelor's degree and became the first Black scholar to receive a Ph.D. from Harvard. His dissertation, *The Suppression of the African Slave Trade*, published in 1896, is a classic historical study. He pursued graduate studies at the University of Berlin, and taught at Wilberforce, the University of Pennsylvania, and Atlanta University. At the same time, he began the enormous literary endeavor that would make him famous as a critic, scholar, editor, and civil rights leader.

Du Bois' educational philosophy revolved around what he called the "Talented Tenth Theory." He advocated a good primary and secondary-school education for Black children of both sexes, of whom the top 10 percent should be encouraged to seek a college education, with generous help from scholarship funds. These young people

BELOW: Dr. Daniel Hale Williams (1856-1931), a pioneer in heart surgery and founder of Provident Hospital in Chicago.

ABOVE: Frances Ellen Harper (1825-1911), a successful author and the most popular Black poet of her time.

BELOW: Mary Church Terrell (1863-1954), civil rights activist and author, was made a member of the school board of the District of Columbia in 1895.

were to be encouraged to go as far as they chose academically, with a strong curriculum grounded in the liberal arts. Ideally, they would become a professional and academic elite equipped to furnish leadership to the entire Black community.

Du Bois' numerous books include *The Philadelphia Negro* (1899), widely considered the first sociological study published by an American; *The Souls of Black Folk* (1903); *John Brown* (1909); *The Negro* (1915); *The Gift of Black Folk* (1924); *Color and Democracy* (1945) and *The World and Africa* (1947). He predicted that the great problem of the twentieth century would be that of the color line between the white nations of the world and the nations compromising the majority "countries of color," and that racial oppression would eventually explode into violence. In 1909 Du Bois helped found the National Association for the Advancement of Colored People (N.A.A.C.P.), in which he was active for most of his life. He edited the organization's magazine, *Crisis*, for 25 years (to 1934). He was an early champion of "Pan-Africanism" and emigrated to Africa in 1961 to work on a major publishing venture pro-

posed by the then president of Ghana, Kwame Nkrumah: the *Encyclopedia Africana*. That same year, disillusioned by the slow pace of change in America, he joined the Communist Party. Du Bois died in Ghana at the age of 95 – on the same day that Martin Luther King, Jr., delivered his famous "I Have a Dream" speech in Washington: August 28, 1963.

Booker T. Washington and W. E. B. Du Bois set the tone and defined the parameters of the debate on civil, political, and economic rights for half a century. A popular poem by Dudley Randall summarizes the differences between them:

Booker T. and W.E.B.
It seems to me, said Booker T,
It shows a mighty lot of cheek
To study chemistry and Greek,
When Mr. Charlie needs a hand
To hoe the cotton on his land
And when Miss Ann looks for a cook,
Why stick your nose inside a book?
I don't agree, said W.E.B.
.If I should have the drive to seek
Knowledge of chemistry or Greek,
I'll do it. Charles and Miss can look
Another place for hand or cook.
Some men rejoice in skill of hand
And some in cultivating land
But there are others who maintain
The right to cultivate the brain.
It seems to me, said Booker T,
That all you folks have missed the boat,
Who shout about the right to vote,
And spend vain days and sleepless
    nights
In uproar over civil rights.
Just keep your mouth shut, and do not
    grouse,
But work, and save, and buy a house.
I don't agree, said W.E.B.
For what can property avail if dignity
    and justice fail?
Unless you help to make the laws,
They'll steal your house with
    trumped-up clause.
A rope's as tight, a fire as hot,
No matter how much cash you've got.
Speak soft and try your little plan,
But as for me I'll be a man.
It seems to me, said Booker T. . . .
I don't agree, said W.E.B.

The First Great Migration: 1910-1930

The twentieth century dawned with the philosophical debate between the Du Bois and Washington factions still raging. It was remarkable how much — and how little — change had occurred since the end of the Civil War. Equally puzzling was the number of African-Americans unaffected by turn-of-the-century shifts in culture and society. Despite marginally better educational opportunities for African-Americans, the general movement to the cities with urban industrialization, and the settling of the West, in which Black soldiers, farmers, and cowboys had participated, fully 80 percent of the Black population remained in 11 of the former Confederate states. Most were in rural areas working as sharecroppers and tenant farmers. Few owned the land that they farmed. A disproportionately large number of African-Americans were still poor, with little prospect for change in the foreseeable future, when the Northern migration got underway. It held out the promise of a different kind of life, with opportunities undreamt of in the South. Yet with it came the pain of separation from one's own environment — community, church, and, often, family. Several organizations sprang up after 1900 to address the needs of Black migrants to Northern cities and the overall question of Black civil rights across the nation.

The Niagara Movement of 1905, founded by Du Bois and William Monroe Trotter, was an all-Black civil rights coalition of intellectuals determined to press for full citizenship rights and public awareness of Black contributions to national stability and progress. By 1909 it was fusing into the National Association for the Advancement of Colored People, which included such White liberals as Oswald Garrison Villard, grandson of abolitionist William

ABOVE: Ben Singleton led a movement of Tennesseeans to settle in Kansas in 1879.

TOP LEFT: Settlers in Nebraska, the Shores family became well-known local musicians.

LEFT: Bill Pickett, one of the Old West's most famous cowboys.

Lloyd Garrison. Its impetus was the economic race riot of 1908 in Springfield, Illinois, which broke out in August near Abraham Lincoln's boyhood home. Many African-Americans had recently moved to the city and were competing with Whites for jobs. A false accusation of a rape by a Black handyman precipitated a riot that left eight Blacks dead and required intervention by the state militia.

In 1911 the National Urban League was founded in New York City by Edmund Haynes and Eugene K. Jones, with support from a number of White benefactors. The League was designed to help Black newcomers to the nation's cities find housing and jobs. Collectively, the new organizations were helping Blacks in urban areas on a short-term basis, but their long-range goals were centered on integration of African-Americans into the mainstream of national life. Meanwhile, the "promised land" proved illusory to many Southern Blacks who had come North in search of greater freedom and prosperity.

In one sense, the African-American migration to Northern cities continued into the 1980s, but historians generally divide the movement into two parts

because of the hiatus created by the Great Depression during the 1930s. The pace picked up again during World War II, when labor shortages and wartime industries created many new jobs. No one could have envisioned these changes at the turn of the century, when the concept of a world war did not exist. But war was only one of several "push" and "pull" forces acting to effect enormous population shifts. The "push" forces were literally pushing Blacks (and poor Whites) off the land in the South. These forces included the destruction of cotton crops by the boll weevil, low pay and land foreclosures, ruinous flooding in 1916, and continuing racial injustice and violence. Between 1900 and 1931, 345 of the South's 551 cotton-growing counties had at least one lynching, and 170 (31 percent) had 10 or more.

The "pull" forces included good wages in war-related Northern industry during World War I. Before the war, Northern factories had exploited the labor of successive waves of European immigrants. This pipeline was all but shut at the very time when cheap labor was badly needed for the war effort. The only place to look was south. Black newspapers like the *Chicago Defender*

LEFT: A shopkeeper in New York City proudly displays a sign that appeared increasingly on small businesses in the twentieth century.

BELOW: A Black foundry worker at Ford's River Rouge plant in 1933.

painted an almost idyllic picture of life in the North, where Blacks could be free of the lynch mob and "live anywhere they wanted." Parents could send their children to good integrated public schools. And you could *vote* in the North.

Some 227,000 Blacks moved north during the decade 1910-20, as opposed to only 79,000 migrants between 1880 and 1910. Between 1920 and 1930, the number reached 440,000. Industrialist George Pullman was paying almost $2 a day at his railroad sleeping-car factory outside Chicago. Steel mills in Gary, Indiana, were paying nearly $1.50 a day. And Henry Ford was reportedly paying the unheard of sum of $5 per day, as compared to 15 to 50 cents per day for Southern farm laborers.

The example of the city of Detroit indicates the level of Black migration into major Northern industrial centers at this time. In 1910 Detroit counted 5,741 African-Americans in its population of 465,766. The city covered 40 square miles of territory. By 1920, the city's population stood at 993,675, of whom 40,838 were Black, and its area had increased to 79.6 square miles. By 1930, when Detroit comprised 140 square miles, there were 120,066 people of

ABOVE: Charles Young (1864-1922) was the third Black graduate from West Point. He fought in the 1898 Spanish-American War and Pershing's 1916 Mexican campaign.

BELOW: Company B of the 25th Infantry in about 1883.

African descent in a population of 1,568,662. Between 1910 and 1920, the city's population and territory increased nearly 300 percent, while its Black population increased by an astonishing 2,400 percent. Cities including Chicago, Cleveland, and Philadelphia saw similar gains in both total and Black populations, as industrial jobs attracted sharecroppers and farm laborers from the South.

Black Soldiers, Sailors, and Veterans

Desite their good record in previous conflicts, including the Spanish-American War, African-Americans practically had to fight their way into the armed forces in 1917-18. It took a wave of protest to overcome initial rejection of Black volunteers for the U.S. Army and Navy (they were not allowed into the U.S. Marines until World War II). Once in the service, most Blacks were assigned to non-combat duty, restricted to training camps, and barred from most clubs for servicemen.

Some African-Americans did see action overseas – fighting in segregated units with White officers. But most Black soldiers didn't fight with their White countrymen; they were assigned to the French Army! The record shows that African-American soldiers fought with distinction, both individually and as a group. Among those singled out for bravery were Privates Needham Roberts and Henry Johnson of the 369th Infantry, who helped hold off a surprise German attack in May 1918, in which both were wounded. The French awarded them the Croix de Guerre. Members of the Black 370th United States Infantry also won commendations for bravery, including the American Distinguished Service Cross and the Croix de Guerre. Meanwhile, at home, race riots were erupting in East St. Louis, Illinois; Houston; Chester, Pennsylvania; and Philadelphia.

Unfortunately, the war brought no end to racism in the U.S.; in fact, it became more virulent. A number of presidents, beginning with Woodrow Wilson, were urged to obtain passage of federal anti-lynching bills, but all were reluctant to bring sufficient pressure to bear on Congress. In the South, the all-White primary continued to disenfranchise Southern Blacks. And in the North, race riots were a constant threat. But African-Americans, especially Black veterans, had changed during the war years. They were demanding greater rights and privileges. Overseas, they had been treated with respect by the French, and a consensus was emerging that they should not settle for less in their own country.

TOP LEFT: Melville Miller, a member of the most famous Black regiment of World War I, the fighting 639th.

ABOVE: In a victory parade in Harlem in 1919 a wounded 369th veteran is greeted by his family.

LEFT: Some officers of the all-Black 92nd ("Buffalo") Division in France in 1918.

ABOVE: The Ku Klux Klan parades in the nation's capital in 1925. Klan membership had grown during the First World War.

RIGHT: A lynch mob in Marion, Indiana, in 1930 proudly displays its bloody handiwork.

But postwar America gave mixed signals at best.

The Ku Klux Klan had experienced a revival during the war years. And most new Klan members lived outside the Southern states. The Klan's resurgence showed increased American intolerance for anyone who differed from the "norm," including Blacks, Catholics, and Jews. Klan terrorism tapped into fear about the spread of Bolshevism (Communism) after the Russian Revolution of 1917. There were 78 lynchings in 1919 – 20 more than the year before, and some of the victims were Black veterans still in uniform. Aliens, dissenters, suspected radicals – all were widely distrusted and became targets of mob violence.

The "Red Summer" of 1919

If the heightened expectations of postwar African-Americans could not be reversed, neither could the increasing conservatism of the larger society. Something had to give. When expectation collided with reality, the result was a summer of violence and bloodshed – what the NAACP's James Weldon Johnson called "the Red Summer." Twenty-five towns and cities were involved. It was the worst year for racial violence in American history and would be until the 1960s.

The riots broke out in both North and South, but they had a number of commonalities. Most were triggered by an incident (or rumor) involving a Black person and a White person, often a Black male and a White female. But in most cases, the underlying cause was White resentment at working with or competing with Blacks for housing and jobs. Some half a million Blacks had migrated North during the war years. Many Southern Whites had also migrated, for the same reasons. They were by no means ready to work side-by-side with a person of color. Clashes were inevitable. In Longview, Texas, White residents were infuriated when they discovered that a local lynching had been reported in the Black newspaper, the *Chicago Defender*. A mob formed to loot Black-owned businesses and attack Black residents, four

White children cheer outside a Black home they have vandalized and set afire during the race riots that swept Chicago in 1919.

of whom were killed. Other riots erupted in Knoxville, Tennessee; Washington, D.C.; and Millen, Georgia, with comparable loss of life.

In Chicago, tension was building on the borders of the Black enclave on the city's South Side, as Black families moved into previously all-White neighborhoods. An estimated 50,000 African-Americans had moved to the city between 1910 and 1920, and White residents were threatening to "bomb them out." This threat was carried out against the homes of 58 African-Americans who attempted to leave their overcrowded neighborhoods. The Chicago riot began on a hot July day at the segregated 29th Street Beach on the South Side. The dividing line down the middle of the beach extended into Lake Michigan. During the course of the day, July 27, a 15-year-old Black swimmer accidentally crossed the line and was stoned by Whites. The youth drowned. When Blacks demanded that the offenders be arrested, the police tried to arrest the Black protesters. Unfounded rumors spread through the city as White youths gathered at so-called athletic clubs from which they headed out to attack unwary Blacks in the downtown area, many returning home from work outside the Black neighborhoods. The city was in the grip

A Chicago policeman kneels beside a Black man beaten in the July 1919 race riots.

3. The commission recommended closing the "athletic clubs" — hangouts used by White rioters as headquarters to coordinate their attacks on innocent citizens.

4. The city government was called upon to upgrade living conditions in African-American neighborhoods. Areas of concern included construction of more schools to end half-day classes at some overcrowded sites. The commission also called for an end to discrimination, desegregation of public facilities, the upgrading of city services in Black neighborhoods, and stricter enforcement of housing and building codes to make dwellings safer.

5. Interestingly, the report blamed the riots in part on a growing sense of "race consciousness" (read "Black Pride") on the part of African-Americans. The commissioners noted that Black people seemed to be more sensitive to racial insults than they had been in the past: this "racial chip" on their shoulders had contributed to the climate of violence. Instrumental in this change of attitude was Marcus Garvey, founder of the United Negro Improve-

of racial violence for almost two weeks, despite the arrival of the National Guard. The melée left 38 dead, 15 Whites and 23 Blacks. More than 500 people were injured. It is hard to believe that only 82 arrests were made by the authorities — seven Whites and 75 Blacks. Of the ten people convicted of crimes during the riot, four were White and six were Black.

The Chicago riot shocked the city and the nation. The governor of Illinois appointed a commission to study its causes and make recommendations. Its findings were published as *The Chicago Riot Report of 1920*, which came to the following conclusions:

1. The police, state militia, courts, and the state's attorneys' office were blamed for a near total breakdown of law and order. These institutions had failed to protect citizens or to arrest and convict the guilty parties.

2. The police were criticized for failing to act quickly to arrest the initial perpetrators at the outset.

ment Association (UNIA) and a charismatic champion of negritude and Pan-Africanism.

Marcus Mosiah Garvey, 1887-1940

Jamaica-born Marcus Garvey is considered the founder of modern-day revolutionary Black Nationalism. A man who spoke no African languages and never set foot on the African continent did more to champion the cause of Pan-Africanism than anyone before or since. He built the largest all-Black civil rights organization in the world on the twin concepts of Black unity and racial pride. Garvey glorified everything Black, from history and culture to physical features. His newspaper, *The Negro World*, accepted no advertisements for what he called "race-degrading" products, including skin lighteners and hair straighteners.

Marcus Garvey arrived in the United States early in 1916, bringing with him the United Negro Improvement Association, which he had founded in Jamaica in 1914. He had read Booker T. Washington's autobiography *Up From Slavery* (and was eager to meet the

author, unaware that Washington had died in late 1915). Garvey settled in New York City's Harlem and traveled the country to convince Black people that they would never enjoy equality until they founded their own nations, industries, and businesses. By 1920 the UNIA claimed nearly two million Black members rallied by the cry "Back to Africa," including people of African descent in Europe, the Caribbean, and other parts of the world. It was the largest international civil rights organization of its kind, and in 1920, it held a 31-day international conclave at Madison Square Garden that proclaimed a formal declaration of Rights for Blacks all over the world.

Garvey's success won him many enemies, and his stay in America was relatively short. Many Black leaders distrusted his rhetoric and his motives. His grandiose business ventures, including the Black Star steamship line, floundered in financial difficulties. His plan for the repatriation of Blacks to

ABOVE: Pan-Africanist Marcus Garvey (1887-1940) in London in 1936, after he had been deported from the United States.

LEFT: A 1930 rally of Marcus Garvey's United Negro Improvement Association in New York City's Harlem.

ABOVE: Dancer Bill (Bojangles) Robinson (1878-1940) and, on the right, bandleader Cab Calloway (1907-) at New York City's Cotton Club.

RIGHT ABOVE: Singer and dancer Josephine Baker (1906-75).

BELOW: Jazz pianist Thomas (Fats) Waller (1904-43).

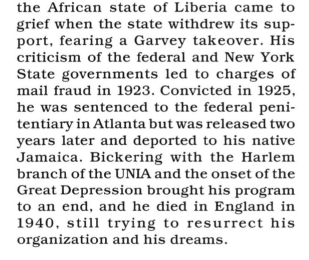

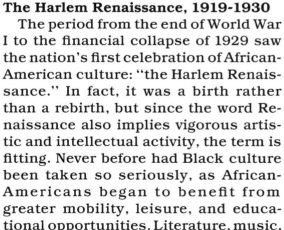

the African state of Liberia came to grief when the state withdrew its support, fearing a Garvey takeover. His criticism of the federal and New York State governments led to charges of mail fraud in 1923. Convicted in 1925, he was sentenced to the federal penitentiary in Atlanta but was released two years later and deported to his native Jamaica. Bickering with the Harlem branch of the UNIA and the onset of the Great Depression brought his program to an end, and he died in England in 1940, still trying to resurrect his organization and his dreams.

The Harlem Renaissance, 1919-1930

The period from the end of World War I to the financial collapse of 1929 saw the nation's first celebration of African-American culture: "the Harlem Renaissance." In fact, it was a birth rather than a rebirth, but since the word Renaissance also implies vigorous artistic and intellectual activity, the term is fitting. Never before had Black culture been taken so seriously, as African-Americans began to benefit from greater mobility, leisure, and educational opportunities. Literature, music, the theater arts – all were enriched by new or newly-recognized contributions from the Black community.

The Harlem Renaissance was an urban movement centered in New York City, the nation's cultural capital.

Spurred on by the debates of Du Bois and Washington, Black intellectuals had become recognizable as a group and were turning to Black culture as a source of solidarity and pride. Musicians like Edward Kennedy "Duke" Ellington and Louis "Satchmo" Armstrong were creating and refining jazz, and William Christopher (W. C.) Handy was composing such classics as "Beale Street Blues" and "Saint Louis Blues." Bessie Smith and other singers brought up on Gospel music took the new sound to a wider audience. Eubie Blake and Noble Sissle made their marks in the world of musical entertainment.

Black writers of the Harlem School were taking indigenous themes and voices that ensured their places in American literature. In 1926 poet Langston Hughes urged fellow Black writers to stop imitating Whites and express themselves honestly. Author Alain Locke called for a literature of art instead of propaganda. Locke's essay *The New Negro* set the tone for the era.

Suddenly, it was fashionable for White New Yorkers to spend an evening

ABOVE: Singer Billie Holiday (1915-59) is introduced to a New Orleans audience in 1946 by bandleader and performer Louis (Satchmo) Armstrong (1900-71).

OPPOSITE BELOW RIGHT: Blues singer Bessie Smith (1894-1937).

LEFT: Bandleader and composer Edward K. (Duke) Ellington (1899-1974) in 1945.

RIGHT: Singer, actor, and activist Paul Robeson (1898-1976), as he looked in 1925.

BELOW: Bandleader and pianist William (Count) Basie (1904-84), left, with author Richard Wright (1908-60) in 1940.

BELOW RIGHT: Poet Langston Hughes (1902-67) in 1925, when he was a hotel busboy in Washington D.C.

uptown in Harlem. Clubs like the Savoy, Small's Paradise, and the Cotton Club catered to White patrons. Composer George Gershwin captured the new awareness of Black America in his acclaimed folk opera *Porgy and Bess*.

On the American stage, actor, singer, and activist Paul Robeson won renown for his work. A graduate of Rutgers University and Columbia University School of Law, he played the male lead in Eugene O'Neill's *All God's Chillun Got Wings* (1924). It was the first time a Black actor had played such a part opposite a White actress. A year later Robeson scored a triumph in O'Neill's *Emperor Jones*. He also made African-American music widely known through his concerts. Ethel Waters was beginning her legendary career on the stage and other noted entertainers of the decade included Bill "Bojangles" Robinson, who costarred in numerous Shirley Temple films, and classical singer Roland Hayes.

Black education and scholarship were also on the ascendant. Carter G. Woodson's Association for the Study of Negro Life and History, founded in 1916, was publishing the *Journal of Negro History*, which still exists today. Anthropologist Zora Neale Hurston wrote about people of African descent in Jamaica and Haiti.

Many accomplishments of the Renaissance period have survived to the present. Unfortunately, much of the movement's fervor abated during the Depression years, only to revive in 1940 with the powerful writings of Richard Wright and Claude McKay, and with such compelling singers as Ella Fitzgerald.

The Great Depression, 1930-1940

The worst economic calamity in the nation's history began with the stock-market collapse of October 1929 and eclipsed all previous depressions in its duration and severity. By this time, millions more were part of the urban-based industrial society, totally dependent on weekly wages for the necessities of life. Hunting, fishing and farming could help feed a hungry family in rural areas, but the urban factory worker was at the mercy of the economy.

For African-Americans the situation was even more critical. "Last hired and first fired" was the attitude of many employers toward Black workers. This was due in part to the fact that Whites took many jobs — the dirtiest, most dangerous, and lowest-paid — formerly held by Blacks. Faced with losing their livelihoods, many White workers gladly accepted such jobs, with the result that Black unemployment in some cities was over 70 percent. The *Chicago Defender* warned its readers to "head for the country before the snow flies." The great Northern migration stalled to a halt during the 1930s. There simply were no jobs.

To make matters even worse, there were no federal programs in place to cushion the initial shock of the Great Depression. There was, for example, no federal insurance on bank deposits; the prosperous 1920s had given the nation a false sense of security. Specu-lation by banks, financiers, and lending institutions had been rampant, and bank failures were widespread. Depositors were fortunate if they could recoup ten cents on the dollar.

Historically, African-Americans had been voting Republican since they gained the franchise after the Civil War. But as the Depression deepened, and Americans looked to the federal government for solutions, it became clear that the Republican administration of Herbert Hoover would do nothing. The president saw the Depression as a product of business and industry shortcomings and expected business and industry to solve the problem — an idea that was both untenable and unacceptable. When the Democratic Party chose Franklin Delano Roosevelt as its candidate in 1932, the stage was set for a major turnaround of the Black vote. Roosevelt's ideas for economic recovery struck a chord in the electorate and won him the

Representative Oscar DePriest and his wife in 1929. DePriest (1871-1951) was then the only Black in the Congress. An Illinois Republican, he served for three terms.

ABOVE: First Lady Eleanor Roosevelt chats with educator and civic leader Mary McLeod Bethune (1875-1955), who then (1937) headed the National Youth Administration and was one of the president's closest advisors.

RIGHT: Singer Marian Anderson (1902-) in her famous 1939 Easter concert given at the Lincoln Memorial. She had been denied the use of Constitution Hall in Washington by the Daughters of the American Revolution.

presidency. His promise of a "New Deal" had a strong appeal for African-Americans, and the appointment of several highly visible Black advisors, known as the "Black Cabinet," was decisive in the Big Switch of Depression politics.

Roosevelt's unofficial Black Cabinet was under the leadership of Mary McLeod Bethune, the youngest of 15 children born to ex-slave parents in South Carolina in 1875. She had received an education through a Quaker benefactor and became a teacher in Sumter, South Carolina, after attending the Moody Bible Institute in Chicago. She married Albertus Bethune and made a name for herself as a woman committed to the well-being of young people in both teaching and government service. President Roosevelt appointed her Director of the Negro Affairs Division of the National Youth Administration in 1935. She also directed the new Office of Minority Affairs. Later she helped found Bethune-Cookman College in Daytona Beach, Florida.

Few members of the Black Cabinet were politicians. Robert L. Vann edited the African-American newspaper, the *Pittsburgh Courier*. Other members included William Hastie of Howard University; Robert Weaver; Eugene Kinckle Jones of the Urban League; and Frank S. Horne, a poet, all of them committed to increasing Black participation in government. Other African-Americans were employed in a variety of fields and departments. In fact, the number of Blacks employed by the federal government rose from 50,000 at Roosevelt's first election in 1932 to nearly 200,000 by the end of World War II. In short, Roosevelt helped African-Americans fight the Depression in a very concrete way—with jobs. As a result, the number of African-Americans voting Democratic rose with each presidential election after 1932. When Roosevelt was elected for an unprecedented fourth term in 1944, the switch was complete. Blacks have given most of their votes to Democratic candidates ever since. In trying to win back the Black vote, the Republicans have had to liberalize many of their policies.

LEFT: Heavyweight boxing champion Sgt. Joe Louis (1911-81) greets WAC volunteers in Chicago in 1944.

BELOW: A World War II poster featuring a wounded Black soldier-turned-war-worker.

The World War II Years and Their Aftermath

By the late 1930s, both Germany and Japan had embarked on courses of conquest and the international scene was ominous. When war broke out in Europe in 1939, U.S. industry experienced a revival that became a massive war effort after Japan attacked the U.S. naval base at Pearl Harbor, Hawaii, on December 7, 1941. With remarkable speed and determination, the nation mobilized.

Despite the national need for man- and womanpower in the defense effort, Blacks were still subject to discrimination. The armed services wanted to enlist them on the basis of their percentage in the population. Companies with defense contracts continued to discriminate against them in both hiring and promotion. In fact, the situation was little changed from that of World War I. Blacks had to threaten the government with protest demonstrations to end bias in war-related industries. A. Philip Randolph, founder and president of the Brotherhood of Sleeping Car Porters and Maids, threatened to lead a march of 100,000 to the nation's capital unless something was done. President Roosevelt finally

TWICE A PATRIOT!

EX-PRIVATE OBIE BARTLETT LOST LEFT ARM—PEARL HARBOR—RELEASED: DEC., 1941—NOW AT WORK WELDING IN A WEST COAST SHIPYARD...

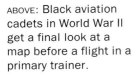

RIGHT: A Black 24-year-old Navy veteran shakes hands with President Roosevelt during World War II.

issued an executive order banning discrimination in war-related industries.

Once again, Black members of the armed forces acquitted themselves admirably. While most American planes never got off the ground during the attack on Pearl Harbor, Black Navy cook Dorie Miller, of the battleship U.S.S. *Arizona*, manned a machine gun and shot down four Japanese planes. He was awarded the Navy Cross. Blacks who wanted to fly fighter planes complained that they were barred from training programs with White pilots. In

ABOVE: Black aviation cadets in World War II get a final look at a map before a flight in a primary trainer.

1940 the War Department agreed to set up a flight school for African-American pilots at Tuskegee, Alabama. A total of 82 such pilots received the Distinguished Flying Cross. For the first time, Black men were accepted into the Marine Corps and Black women into the WAVES (Women Accepted for Volunteer Emergency Service), a branch of the U.S. Navy.

Over 1,000,000 African-American men and women were inducted into the armed forces during the war. Of that number approximately 500,000 served overseas. For the first time in any war, African-Americans served in all branches of the armed services including the Coast Guard; they also entered the Merchant Marine. As in World War I, many were assigned to non-combat duties, while others saw combat and won medals for bravery from their country and its allies.

On the down side, the nation suffered its worst race riot of the century to that point. African-American migration had reached unprecedented numbers in the wake of labor shortages in war-related industries. Housing had become a critical issue, along with tension at the workplace, between Black and White workers. In June 1943, a race riot erupted in Detroit, at a park on the Detroit River. When the violence finally subsided, 34 persons were dead.

Postwar Changes

The end of World War II saw permanent change in many areas of American life. The migration of African-Americans from the rural South to urban areas, especially in the North, had resumed after the lull caused by the Great Depression. The 1950 census reported net 10-year Black emigration from the South at 1.6 million. Detroit's

Black population went from some 120,000 in 1940 to more than 300,000 by 1950. Chicago had 233,000 residents of African descent in 1940 and almost 500,000 a decade later. The war years had continued the process of turning the Black population from a rural proletariat into an urban industrial working class. By the 1950s Blacks were more educated and better paid than at any time before, especially in the North. They were more sophisticated and knowledgeable about the world beyond the United States. Black veterans of two wars had helped create an international perspective for all the residents of the community.

While life in the cities offered more opportunities, it was creating a new Black culture. Urban Blacks still found themselves living in Black ghettoes — not necessarily in run-down housing, but with few choices outside the Black

ABOVE: Police lead an injured Black away from the scene of a race riot that took place in New York's Harlem in 1943.

LEFT: Jim Crowism in action: a segregated drinking fountain in Oklahoma in 1939.

neighborhoods. On the other hand, such large concentrations of Blacks had unexpected benefits. The Black communities in many Northern cities had grown big enough to create predominately Black congressional districts. By the mid-1950s there were Black representatives in Congress from New York City, Chicago, and Detroit. Debate among the various civil rights organizations looked toward removing the legal barriers to the ending of segregation.

The National Association for the Advancement of Colored People had become the premier civil rights organization by the fifth decade of the century. It decided to make an all-out assault on *de jure* (by law) segregation. After years of attacking the doctrine of "separate but equal," NAACP lawyers were encouraged when the U.S. Supreme Court asked to re-hear five school segregation cases first heard in 1942. On May 17, 1954, by a unanimous 9 to 0 vote, the Supreme Court ruled that "separate but equal" educational facilities were "inherently unequal" and that segregation was unconstitutional. This decision in the case of *Brown v. Board of Education* (of Topeka, Kansas) overturned the doctrine that had legitimized segregation since the *Plessy* decision of 1896.

ABOVE: Segregation at the University of Oklahoma in 1948: an elderly Black student is not allowed to sit in the same classroom with White students.

RIGHT: A Black school in rural Georgia in the early 1940s.

ABOVE: Blacks line up outside the Supreme Court Building on the day in 1952 when the Court is scheduled to begin hearing some suits that challenge school segregation. One of them is *Brown v. Board of Education of Topeka*.

LEFT: The victorious attorneys in the High Court's landmark 1954 *Brown* decision. In the middle is future Supreme Court Justice Thurgood Marshall (1908-1993).

Chapter Six

RIGHT: Roy Wilkins (1901-81) receives congratulations on being named executive secretary of the NAACP in 1955.

BELOW: Statesman and scholar Ralph Bunche (1904-71) autographs programs in Oslo, Norway, in 1950 after winning the Nobel Peace Prize. He was the first African-American so honored.

The years between the *Brown* case in 1954 and 1972 have often been called the Second Reconstruction, and the similarities between the two periods are noteworthy. Both saw African-Americans make tremendous gains in the fields of politics and civil rights. Both occurred after the enactment of major legislation that permanently altered race relations: the Thirteenth Amendment, which ended slavery, and the Supreme Court decision that outlawed school segregation. But there were significant differences as well.

The years 1954-72 saw two different ideologies debated and adopted by African-Americans. The term "Civil Rights era" is most accurately applied to the period between 1954 and the mid-1960s, marked by peaceful protests that used non-violent tactics even when demonstraters met violent oppo-

sition. This movement was largely led by an older generation of African-Americans and was centered in the South. Its leaders used the laws, and usually remained within the laws, to achieve their goals.

By the mid-1960s this approach yielded to something quite different. A significant rift had occurred within the movement on the question of strategy, tactics, and goals. The resultant Black Power movement took root in urban centers and lasted until the early years of the 1970s. There was "change within change," and America would never be the same.

The Second Reconstruction, 1954-1972

The Civil Rights Movement, 1954 to 1964

A precise date or event for the beginning of the Civil Rights movement is open to debate. Some people use the *Brown* decision as the precipitating event; others see the Montgomery, Alabama, bus boycott of 1955-56 as the starting point. Others point farther back, to the World War II experience. While a case can be made for all three, the first two events were the most obvious and immediate.

The pace of desegregation after the Supreme Court called for "all deliberate speed" varied from town to town and state to state. The only constant was that the rate of compliance was generally slow. The ruling was aimed specifically at the nation's public school system, but African-Americans and most civil rights organizations pushed for a wider interpretation. Black people in the South wanted to see an end not only to school segregation but to all segregation, which was still endemic. This was the impetus for the Montgomery bus boycott.

In 1955 Montgomery, the capital of Alabama, was a segregated city with a sizable African-American population. One of the most visibly segregated institutions was the city bus system. A sign of demarcation divided White passengers in the front from Black passengers in the rear. African-Americans boarded the bus at the front to pay their fare, then had to get off and reboard at the rear entrance. If this weren't galling enough, the dividing line between the

LEFT: "Uncle Mose" Wright, grand-uncle of slain Emmett Till, identifies two of the boy's murderers in court in a sensational trial in Mississippi in 1955. A 14-year-old Black, Till had been lynched for whistling at a White woman.

BELOW: The all-White male jury at the Till murder trial listens to the evidence. Only two of the alleged lynchers had been charged, and the jury would acquit both.

ABOVE: Rosa Parks (1913-). Her arrest for defying segregated seating on a bus in Montgomery, Alabama, provoked a 1956 Black boycott of city buses.

BELOW: The Rev. Martin Luther King, Jr., was one of the leaders of the Montgomery boycott.

White and Black sections could be changed to suit White needs.

If a White passenger couldn't find a seat in the front, he could demand the seat of a Black. But if the Black section was overcrowded and there were empty seats in the White section, Black passengers had to stand. The line of demarcation moved only one way — to the back. Black citizens had hoped that the city would voluntarily desegregate the bus system. When it didn't happen, they prepared to take action.

The Montgomery bus boycott of 1955-56 launched a young minister into the headlines, but Martin Luther King, Jr., was not the one who began the protest. That honor goes to a gentleman whose identity was obscured by the publicity process: Mr. Edward Daniel (E. D.) Nixon. Mr. Nixon was a retired member of the Brotherhood of Sleeping Car Porters and Maids and was probably influenced by the tactics of the union's radical leader, A. Philip Randolph. Nixon was also the president of the Montgomery chapter of the NAACP, of which Mrs. Rosa Parks was the secretary. Together they came up with the idea of protesting Montgomery's segregation laws. When Mrs. Parks took a seat at the front of the Cleveland Avenue bus and refused to give it up to a White passenger, she was arrested. Nixon used this incident to challenge the city's segregation laws and invited the young Reverend Martin Luther King, Jr., to be the spokesman for the protest.

The Montgomery bus boycott began on December 5, 1955, and ended successfully a year later. During the interim, African-Americans simply refused to ride city busses. Instead, Montgomery's Black community formed its own transportation system. Under the banner of the Montgomery Improvement Association, Black residents organized car pools and started an ad hoc taxicab company. Many traveled on foot throughout the year. African-Americans who didn't own cars used the car pools, hitchhiked, rode bicycles, or hiked to their destinations. Late in 1956 the Supreme Court ruled that segregated public transportation was unconstitutional.

In the end, the city relented. Since African-Americans comprised nearly one-third of the population, the municipal bus line faced going out of business if the boycott continued.

King gained national recognition as spokesman for the protest and went on to become the preeminent leader of the Civil Rights movement. But if Rosa Parks is considered the mother of the movement, Edward D. Nixon should properly be called its father. By the fall

of 1956 some 800 Southern school districts, with 320,000 Black children, had desegregated. However, almost 2.5 million Black children remained in segregated schools, including those in Virginia, North and South Carolina, Georgia, Florida, Mississippi, Alabama, and Louisiana. The Deep South had dug in to fight integration. When Black student Autherine Lucy was admitted to the University of Alabama by court order, riots ensued, and she was expelled on a technicality. In Congress, Southern senators, led by Harry Byrd of Virginia, obtained the signatures of 100 congressmen to a "Southern Manifesto" that attacked the Supreme Court. Lyndon B. Johnson was among the Southern lawmakers who refused to sign the document.

In 1957 President Dwight D. Eisenhower ordered federal troops to Little Rock, Arkansas, to enforce an order for integration of 18 Black pupils into Central High School. Tennessee announced that desegregation of state universities would begin in 1958, and the Southern Christian Leadership Conference was formed by Martin Luther King, Jr., Bayard Rustin, and Stanley Levinson to coordinate the activities of nonviolent groups working toward integration and full citizenship for Blacks. The following year, Black voter registration rose slowly, as the Southern states instituted complicated delaying tactics. In Mississippi only three percent of eligible Blacks were registered to vote. The state's White Citizens Councils exerted economic pressure on potential Black voters, including denial of the customary pre-harvest loans, while more extreme groups resorted to terrorism.

After the Montgomery boycott, and Little Rock, the Civil Rights movement was constantly in the news. In 1960 the forces of protest were galvanized by the "sit-in" movement, which began in Greensboro, North Carolina. Four Black students from North Carolina Agricultural and Technical College sat down at the segregated lunch counter of the local Woolworth department store and refused to move when they were refused service. The national

LEFT: Daisy Bates (1922-) was president of the Arkansas NAACP during the 1958 school segregation crisis in Little Rock, Arkansas, and one of the heroines of that key episode in civil rights history.

BELOW: Jeered by White students, Elizabeth Eckford tries to pass through a cordon of National Guardsmen to gain entrance to the Central High School in Little Rock in 1957.

media picked up the story and inspired other students at historically Black colleges and universities across the South. So many rushed to join the protest movement that the Student Non-Violent Coordinating Committee (SNCC) was formed in Atlanta later that year. It wasn't long before Black and White students from Northern colleges were going South to participate in the protests, many of them trained in the techniques of passive resistance by the Congress of Racial Equality (CORE). Sit-ins spread to Nashville, Montgomery, and other cities. Before the year was out, lunch counters in Greensboro, San Antonio, and other communities were desegregated. Church kneel-ins and beach wade-ins joined lunch-counter and bus-station sit-ins, and public awareness of the depth and scope of racism in America spread more widely than ever before. In 1960 the Democratic candidate for president, John F. Kennedy, received two-thirds of the Black vote and won a very close election. That same year, A. Philip Randolph formed the Negro-

American Labor Council to counter what he saw as lip service to union desegregation by the AFL-CIO. And the first Northern integration suit occurred when Black parents sued to end *de facto* segregation in the schools of New Rochelle, New York, a suburb of New York City. The case was won the following year.

In 1961 several busloads of Freedom Riders organized by CORE set out on a ride through the South to test the compliance of bus lines with the desegregation order issued by the Interstate Commerce Commission in 1955. Many of them were arrested and attacked. Attorney General Robert F. Kennedy ordered 600 U.S. marshals to Montgomery to maintain order. Six more states passed laws forbidding segregation in housing, bringing the U.S. total to 10. Some progress was seen in the federal government when Black congressman Adam Clayton Powell, Jr., was named chairman of the House Education and Labor Committee and James P. Parsons was appointed the first Black federal district judge.

ABOVE: U.S. Attorney General Robert Kennedy talks to civil rights marchers in Washington in 1963. Although he decried discrimination in hiring, he refused to endorse the idea of affirmative action.

LEFT: White "Freedom Rider" James Zwerg in Montgomery in 1961, after a beating by pro-segregationists. No White ambulance in town would take him to the hospital.

121

RIGHT: Civil rights worker James Meredith (1933-). In 1961-62 he was denied entry to the University of Mississippi, despite a U.S. Supreme Court ruling in his favor. U.S. marshals had to escort him to class.

BELOW: The burnt hulk of a Freedom Riders' bus, torched by a mob of segregationists in Alabama in 1961.

A year after serviceman Fred Moore became the first black sentry to guard the Tomb of the Unknown Soldier, the Kennedy administration ordered military commanders actively to oppose discriminatory practices in the armed forces. In 1962 the U.S. Army reported that 3 percent of its officers and 12 percent of its enlisted men were Black. The U.S. Navy had even lower figures: only 5 percent of its enlisted men were Black and none of its officers (3 percent) was a ship commander. That year Samuel L. Gravely was appointed commander of the destroyer escort U.S.S. *Falgout*. Later, he would become the first Black American admiral.

In mid-September 1962, President Kennedy denounced the burning of churches in Georgia to discourage Black voter registration drives and assured governmental protection of those seeking to exercise their voting rights. Only two weeks later, riots occurred at the University of Mississippi in Oxford when several hundred U.S. marshals escorted James Meredith to the campus to register as the school's first black student. The rioting was quelled only with the aid of some 3,000 U.S. soldiers and federalized National Guardsmen.

Nineteen-sixty-three proved to be a watershed year for the Civil Rights Movement — a year of both great adversity and renewed determination. In Jackson, Mississippi, Medgar Evers, NAACP field secretary and a prominent civil rights leader, was assassinated in the doorway of his home. In April a major civil rights campaign against segregation in Birmingham, led by Martin Luther King, Jr., began in Alabama. Within three weeks, more than 400 protesters had been arrested. The police used dogs against the protesters beginning on May 2, and city firemen turned high-pressure firehoses on them. By May 7, 2,500 demonstraters had been arrested, many of them children. The May 11 bombings of a Black leader's home and of a desegregated motel caused reassignment of federal troops to bases near Birmingham by President Kennedy. A month later, Alabama governor George Wallace defied a presidential order to register two Black students at the state university. He yielded only after Kennedy federalized the Alabama National Guard.

Famed TV journalist Charlayne Hunter-Gault first made headlines in 1961 by becoming one of the first two Blacks admitted to a Georgia public school — in this case the University of Georgia. She wrote about the experience in a book published in 1993.

RIGHT: George Wallace, governor of Alabama, personally blocks the entry of Blacks into the University of Alabama in 1967. They entered anyway, with the help of the now-federalized National Guard of Alabama.

FAR RIGHT: The first Black admitted to a South Carolina public school, Harvey Garitt enters Clemson in 1963.

RIGHT: Demonstrators in Birmingham, Alabama, in 1963 hold hands to prevent being knocked down by water from police firehoses.

OPPOSITE: In 1963 a young demonstrator in Birmingham kneels in tearful prayer.

ABOVE: Commissioner of Police Eugene "Bull" Connor and some of his Birmingham officers. Connor's brutal means of dealing with civil rights demonstrators shocked TV viewers and won much sympathy for the cause of the Black desegregationists.

RIGHT: Governor Ross Barnett (right, with glasses) personally denies James Meredith entry to University of Mississippi grounds in September 1962.

On August 28, 1963, the largest demonstration ever seen in Washington, D.C., converged on the Capitol: some 250,000 civil rights activists, Black and White, demanded full civil rights for Blacks in the historic march on Washington. It was led by Martin Luther King, Jr., whose commitment to nonviolent resistance began in his youth. He came from a respected family of Baptist ministers in Atlanta, Georgia, and studied for the ministry at Crozier Theological Seminary and Boston University. At the Lincoln Memorial, he delivered his "I Have a Dream" address,

which moved the conscience of the nation. The following year he would receive the Nobel Prize for Peace and the Kennedy Peace Prize.

Not all Americans were moved by the march on Washington. Three weeks later, a bomb exploded in Birmingham's 16th Street Baptist Church, killing four children and injuring 20 others. The riot that ensued had to be quelled by the National Guard and state troopers. At this time, less than 10 percent of Southern Black children were attending integrated schools. The assassination of President Kennedy in

The Rev. Martin Luther King, Jr., standing before the portraits of three civil rights workers murdered in Mississippi a few weeks earlier, speaks to CORE demonstrators in August 1964.

127

Dallas that November closed the year on a tragic note. Lyndon B. Johnson succeeded him, with a promise to support strong civil rights legislation.

The transition from non-violent to Black-power activism became apparent in 1964, when Black Muslim leader Malcolm X resigned from the movement to form the Organization for Afro-American Unity. This was in the wake of the July 18 race riot in New York City's Harlem, in which one person was killed, almost 150 were injured, and 500 arrested in what proved to be the first of many such riots in Northern urban ghettoes. The rioting soon spread to Brooklyn's Bedford-Stuyvesant section, several New Jersey cities, Chicago, and Philadelphia. Only a month before, three young civil rights workers, James Chaney, a Black, and Whites Michael Schwerner and Andrew Goodman, had been murdered in Philadelphia, Mississippi. Among the 19 suspects were the sheriff and a deputy sheriff of Neshoba County. There were

OPPOSITE TOP: Martin Luther King, Jr. delivers his moving "I Have a Dream" speech to civil rights marchers in Washington, D.C., on August 28, 1963.

OPPOSITE BOTTOM: At the Lincoln Memorial on August 28, 1963, (from left) Burt Lancaster, Harry Belafonte, and Charlton Heston chat before entertaining the crowd of marchers.

ABOVE LEFT: More than 200,000 people took part in the August 28, 1963, civil rights march on Washington.

LEFT: Another scene of Washington, D.C., on August 28, 1963: marchers en route to the Lincoln Memorial from the Washington Monument.

LEFT: The scene as Dr. King saw it when he delivered the "I Have a Dream" speech.

TOP: Marchers shake Dr. King's hand in the aftermath of his most famous speech.

ABOVE: The rapt faces of Dr. King's audience during the "I Have a Dream" speech.

no convictions, and the charges would be dismissed in December. Sadly, the urban rioting followed closely upon enactment of a major civil rights bill: The Civil Rights Act of 1964, which forbade discrimination in public accommodations, employment, and many other socioeconomic spheres.

The following year, the Voting Rights Act of 1965 was enacted, and the national media spurred public debate on civil and human rights, militancy, and the emergent Black Power movement. In January, Martin Luther King, Jr., announced that he would call for demonstrations if Alabama Blacks were restrained from registering and voting. A month later, he and 770 other Blacks were arrested in Selma and jailed for four days, during which 3,000 other persons were arrested. A federal district court ordered the county board of registrars to refrain from complicating the registration process so as to deny Blacks the right to vote.

King and thousands of protesters undertook the five-day, fifty-four-mile march from Selma to the state capital of Montgomery on March 7, to dramatize the denial of voting rights to Blacks. The first attempt to march was halted

ABOVE: Dr. King leads civil rights marchers on the first leg of their celebrated 1965 march from Selma to Montgomery, Alabama.

RIGHT: A woman marcher injured by Alabama state troopers during the Selma-Montgomery march in 1965.

by 200 Alabama state troopers and possemen of the Dallas County Sheriff's Office, who attacked the demonstraters with tear gas, nightsticks, and whips on grounds that Governor Wallace had banned the demonstration. It was finally carried out between March 21 and 25, after federal judge Frank M. Johnson, Jr., enjoined Governor Wallace and other state officials from intimidating the participants.

Components of the Black Power Movement

Though the Civil Rights and Black Power movements overlapped for some years, they were strikingly different in their venues, goals, leadership, tactics, and results. Northern Blacks found themselves segregated, too, primarily by custom rather than by law. This *de facto* segregation was, in many ways, harder to do away with than were discriminatory laws, which could be — and were being — struck down. Thus the riots in non-Southern cities, beginning with the Watts riot in Los Angeles in 1965, were fueled largely by frustration — not only at racism, but at the lack of an easily identifiable target at which to strike back.

ABOVE: Dr. King with Malcolm X (1925-65), the most famous of Black Muslims and a fiery proponent of Black Power. The two leaders differed on matters of tactics.

LEFT: A Black Muslim holds up a newspaper showing a picture of Elijah Muhammad (1896-1975), founder of the Nation of Islam faith.

ABOVE: Malcolm X was at first militantly anti-White, urging Blacks to use "any means necessary" to end oppression, and espousing the cause of Black Nationalism. He later moderated his view somewhat.

Battlegrounds for the Black Power movement were primarily in Northern cities. Its goal was the "decolonization" of the Black community rather than integration into the larger society. Exploitation of Black labor and economic inequality were major sources of resentment. Black Power advocates wanted African-Americans to control the politics, economics, educational facilities, and other institutions within the Black community. The new tactics were summed up in Malcolm X's phrase, "by any means necessary." Non-violence was not ruled out, but violent conflict was an acceptable means to the desired end.

The new leaders were, as a group, younger and more militant than those of the Civil Rights Movement. Many were college students or recent graduates. The "big three" were Malcolm X of the Black Muslims/Nation of Islam, Stokely Carmichael of SNCC and the Black Panther Party, and H. Rap Brown of SNCC. Stokely Carmichael has been credited with inventing the term "Black Power," although New York congressman Adam Clayton Powell had used it

RIGHT: New York City police carry the body of Malcolm X away from the Audubon Ballroom in Harlem, where he was murdered by dissident Blacks at a political rally on February 21, 1965.

in the 1950s. Young militant H. Rap Brown sent shock waves through the nation when he cried, "Burn, baby, burn" in the wake of urban riots. Both Carmichael and Brown were still in their twenties.

Where the Civil Rights Movement had identified racism on the part of individuals as the major problem, Black Power advocates saw institutional racism as "the Enemy." The problem was not so much ignorant or bigoted people as corrupt institutions, including most of the social-political-economic system. Thus the problem with an incident like the attempted integration of the University of Alabama in 1956 was redefined. It didn't matter whether or not Black students were in attendance at the university: the problem was what that university, and by extension all universities, were teaching.

African-American college students played an important part in the Black Power Movement, as they had in the cause of civil rights. The focus shifted to Northern campuses, where most students were White, and included demands for courses in Black studies,

separate cultural facilities, and even separate living quarters. Black Student Unions were formed to coordinate activities, most of which barred Whites from membership.

Urban police forces were viewed mainly as "armies of occupation" in the ghettoes and were, with non-Black merchants, the most frequent targets of race-riot violence.

One positive result of the Black Power Movement was a great increase in Black racial pride, symbolized by the phrase, "Black Is Beautiful." African-Americans began to dress in African clothes and to wear their hair in "Afro" styles. The term "Black" began to replace "colored" or "Negro," which many found unacceptable.

The Black Nationalist Movement suffered a heavy blow when 39-year-old Malcolm X was shot to death on February 21, 1965, as he was about to address a New York City rally. Black Muslims were the immediate suspects, since they had suspended Malcolm X in 1963, after he referred to President Kennedy's assassination as the case of "chickens coming home to roost."

Representative Adam Clayton Powell (1908-72) addresses Blacks in the Watts section of Los Angeles in 1968. Three years earlier, Watts was the scene of one of the worst race riots in U.S. history.

Black Muslim headquarters in New York City and San Francisco were burned after the murder, and Muslim leaders were closely watched. (Ultimately, three of them were convicted of the murder and sentenced to life imprisonment.)

In August 1965, a major race riot broke out in the Watts area of Los Angeles. Urban Blacks, protesting police brutality, looted and burned stores and other buildings, resulting in 35 deaths and property damage estimated at $200 million. High unemployment was cited as a major factor.

In June 1966, James Meredith was shot and wounded in Mississippi during a 200-mile walk to encourage unregistered Blacks to vote. A coalition of Non-Violent and Black Power factions finished the march; it proved an uneasy alliance and revealed the tensions between the two civil rights groups. A month later, another summer of urban race riots began with gunfire, looting of stores, and fire-bombing on Chicago's West Side. The hot

weather, lack of recreational facilities, unemployment, and degraded living conditions were all seen as contributors to the violence, which spread to Cleveland, Brooklyn, Omaha, Baltimore, San Francisco, and Jacksonville.

In July 1967, race riots erupted in Newark, New Jersey, leaving 26 dead and more than 1,500 injured. A week later, the Detroit riot broke out and raged for eight days, leaving at least 40 dead, 2,000 injured, and 5,000 homeless as a result of arson and looting. On July 24 President Johnson called in 4,700 federal paratroopers aided by 8,000 National Guardsmen (the first time in 24 years that federal forces had been used to quell civil disorders). Property damage was estimated at between $250 and $400 million. Seven months later, the Kerner Commission's "Report on Civil Disorders" cited White racism as the chief cause of Black violence and riots. Unemployment, inadequate housing, and discriminatory police practices were called contributing factors.

Even larger than the Watts riots were the Detroit riots of 1967: 43 dead, 7,200 under arrest, and at least $40 million worth of property damage.

On April 4, 1968, Martin Luther King, Jr., was killed by sniper James Earl Ray in Memphis, Tennessee, where the civil rights leader was meeting with activists Jesse Jackson and Ralph Abernathy. A wave of shock and grief set off Black rioting and looting across the nation. A month later, Abernathy led the King-planned Poor People's March on Washington, D.C. The following January, a series of student riots closed many college campuses, as Black and White students made common cause in opposing the war in Vietnam. Black students demanded Black Studies programs and open admission policies, while White radical students were more concerned with ending ROTC and Dow Chemical recruiting on campus.

Roman Catholic bishops had called on church members to "declare war" on racism in housing, education, and employment in 1968. From this point, Black Catholics would be a much more visible and vocal presence on the American religious scene.

ABOVE: On April 3, 1968, Martin Luther King, Jr. stands on the Memphis Motel balcony where he would be murdered the next day. Flanking him are Jesse Jackson (left) and Ralph Abernathy.

LEFT: A mule-drawn caisson carries the body of Martin Luther King,Jr., slain on April 4, 1968 by White assassin James Earl Ray.

ABOVE: Adam Clayton Powell listens as SNCC chairman Stokely Carmichael (1944-) answers questions from reporters at a 1966 press conference.

TOP RIGHT: Eldridge Cleaver (1935-), one of the most militant of the Black Panther Party, was constantly in conflict with the police.

RIGHT: Black Panthers march in New York City in 1968 in support of Panther leader Huey Newton, held in Los Angeles, CA, on a murder charge.

The Black Panther Movement had come into the public eye in 1967, when member Huey P. Newton was tried and convicted of manslaughter in the fatal shooting of a white patrolman. A year later, Eldridge Cleaver, the Black Panthers' Minister of Information, was sought by police as a parole violator on a fugitive warrant issued in San Francisco. In December 1968, three members of the Panthers were arrested on charges of carrying out a machine-gun attack on a Jersey City police station. Wholesale accusations on both sides made it difficult to sort out fact from fiction in the ensuing media blitz.

Nineteen-sixty-nine brought widespread disorders in the Black neighborhoods of Hartford, Connecticut, after a summer of comparative peace. Firebombings and snipings brought on a dusk-to-dawn curfew in the Connecticut capital. In September, a report by the U.S. Commission on Civil Rights, chaired by the Reverend Theodore Hesburgh of the University of Notre Dame, charged the administration of Richard M. Nixon with choosing the wrong school desegregation policy and supporting it with inflated statistics.

ABOVE: In 1968, Olympic athletes Tommie Smith and John Carlos give the Black Power salute when presented with awards in Mexico City.

LEFT: The shattered wall of a dormitory at predominanly Black Jackson State College, Mississippi, where, in May 1970, two Black youths were shot down by police in a still-unexplained eruption of violence.

School integration still lagged far behind the program envisioned for almost 20 years. In April 1971, the Supreme Court upheld bussing as the primary means of achieving it. When the new school year opened in the fall, bussing was countered by demonstrations and violence in both the North and the South.

The period between 1971 and 1975 was one of contrasts and contradictions. There were many more Black officeholders than at any time in American history, many of them from areas where Whites comprised a majority, yet political leaders as a group were increasingly cool to the demands of the Black electorate. Opposition to school integration spread from the South to the North, and within the Black community, but more Blacks than ever were attending integrated schools and colleges. Some politicians appealed to the fears and prejudices of White voters, and extra-legal action by the police against Black citizens was often reported, if seldom proved and punished by the courts. Yet African-Americans were increasingly united in presenting their demands and expressing pride in their ethnic and cultural heritage. This new unity was manifested at the Gary Convention of 1972, where Coretta King, widow of the Reverend Martin Luther King, Jr., and Bobby Seale of the Black Panthers sat together on the podium.

ABOVE: Roy Innis (1934-), just-elected national director of CORE, outlines new policies at a meeting in St. Louis in 1968.

LEFT: Attorney William Kunstler addresses a group of supporters of H. Rap Brown, jailed on charges of riot and arson, in 1970. Brown (1943-) then headed the SNCC.

OPPOSITE: In 1975 the NAACP held a "National March on Boston" to commemorate the 21st anniversary of the Supreme Court's *Brown* decision. Some 7,000 people took part.

Chapter Seven

The Civil Rights Movement had culminated in passage of the Civil Rights and Voting acts of 1964/65. These measures would give Southern Blacks full rights of citizenship for the first time. Not only could they expect to vote without fearing for their lives, they could run for and hold elected office to an extent never possible before. African-Americans in the South could see real changes as a result of the protests, with middle-class or would-be middle-class Blacks benefiting the most. Those with political skills were empowered to exercise them.

Andrew Young, for example, who started as an advisor to Martin Luther King, Jr., went on to represent his Atlanta district in Congress and then to become mayor of Atlanta. Other Blacks, both men and women, entered the political arena for the first time.

On the down side, the Civil Rights Movement had a less immediate effect on African-Americans outside the South, especially in Northern cities, and on those living in poverty nationwide. Mounting frustration among these groups led to formation of the Black Power Movement.

The violent confrontations of the late 1960s saw excesses on both sides and deplorable losses of life and property. Ultimately, the goals of Black Nationalism were not only unachievable, but unacceptable to many members of the Black community, as well as the White majority. However, the Black Power Movement had the positive effect of increasing racial pride and solidarity. Political consciousness was raised,

Today and Tomorrow

In fact, by 1980, New York and Chicago had one-tenth of the nation's Black population. Many other cities now have African-American majorities, including Detroit (80 percent); Oakland, California; Newark, New Jersey; Gary, Indiana; New Orleans, Atlanta, and Washington, D.C. Five of the six largest cities have or have had Black mayors in the last 30 years, including New York City (David Dinkins), Chicago (the late Harold Washington), Los Angeles (Thomas Bradley), Philadelphia (Wilson Goode) and Detroit (Coleman Young).

At the state level, several Black governors and lieutenant-governors have taken office since the 1960s, including L. Douglas Wilder, elected governor of Virginia in 1989.

The national level has seen significant changes and gains in the past 30

LEFT: David Dinkins (1927-) became the first Black mayor of New York City. He is seen here with his wife at his victory celebration in 1989.

BELOW: In 1966 Edward Brooke (1919-) became the first Black to be elected to the U.S. Senate since the days of Reconstruction. He served two terms as a Republican Senator from Massachusetts.

and government began to address more of the concerns facing African-Americans in Northern cities and suburbs. However, the results fell far short of the movement's goals, and it began to wane in the early 1970s.

On balance, it was too much to expect that the problems of more than 300 years would be solved in two short decades. But real progress had been made between 1954 and 1974, and that progress has continued into the present. Who would have believed, in the days of firehoses, tear gas, and police dogs, that Birmingham, Alabama, would elect a Black mayor? But that is just what happened.

New York City now has more Black residents than any city in the nation.

RIGHT: Jazz trumpeter and bandleader John (Dizzy) Gillespie (1917-1993) performs in Holland in 1990.

BELOW RIGHT: Singer Whitney Houston wins a Grammy Award for "I Wanna Dance with Somebody" in 1988.

BELOW: Rev. Barbara Harris (1931-) was made the first female Anglican bishop in February 1989.

years. In 1988 the Reverend Jesse L. Jackson launched his second run for the presidency. Though scoffed at by many political pundits, Jackson mounted a credible campaign by winning four Democratic state primaries. In 1989 General Colin Powell became the first African-American appointed chairman of the Joint Chiefs of Staff of the U.S. armed services. African-Americans have held cabinet posts under every president since Lyndon Johnson. Robert C. Weaver assumed leadership of the newly created Department of Housing and Urban Development in 1965. During the Carter Administration, Patricia Roberts Harris became the first African-American woman appointed to a cabinet post. She served as secretary of Housing and Urban Development and later as secretary of Health, Education, and Welfare.

ABOVE: Charles Dutton, star of the Fox Television comedy *Roc*, has also starred in Hollywood films and such Broadway productions as the Pulitzer Prize-winning *The Piano Lesson* (1990).

TOP LEFT: Superstar Michael Jackson (r.) with talk show host Oprah Winfrey.

In 1983 President Ronald Reagan signed a bill declaring a national holiday in honor of Dr. Martin Luther King, Jr. The 1992 elections saw Black Americans elected to Congress in greater numbers than ever before .

Today Black entertainers and athletes enjoy unprecedented acceptance and command huge salaries. Michael Jackson, Bill Cosby, Richard Pryor, Tina Turner, Whitney Houston, director Spike Lee, Denzel Washington — these are only a few of the major show-business personalities. On the athletic field, football stars include Jerry Rice of the San Francisco '49ers, Emmett Smith of the Dallas Cowboys, Lawrence Taylor of the New York Giants, and Art Monk and Gary Clark of the Washington Redskins. Black quarterback Doug Williams led the Redskins to a Superbowl championship in 1988.

Black athletes dominate every playing position in professional basketball but there are still only a half-dozen Black coaches. Names like Earvin "Magic" Johnson and Michael Jordan have gained the same recognition as that enjoyed by Norman "Wilt" Chamberlain — still the only professional to score 100 points in a single game. Black dominance of college bas-

BOTTOM LEFT: Chuck Berry (1926-) holds a Grammy Lifetime Achievement Award.

BELOW: Laker great Wilt Chamberlain just before his retirement in 1973.

ABOVE: Pro football and baseball star Bo Jackson in his first at bat for the Chicago White Sox, September 2, 1991.

TOP RIGHT: The world heavyweight boxing champion in 1973-74, George Foreman made unsuccessful comeback bids in 1981 and 1990.

ketball has been apparent since 1965, when Texas Western University (now the University of Texas at El Paso), a predominantly White college, became the first school to win the NCAA basketball championship with an all-Black starting lineup. Their opponents, the University of Kentucky, fielded an all-White team. (This was also the last time a college basketball team made it to the finals without at least one African-American player.)

The number of Black college students has doubled since the 1960s, to almost one million, of whom almost 75 percent are in predominantly White colleges. With the help of affirmative action initiatives, and as colleges move to diversify their student bodies and

faculties, the opportunities for African-Americans have improved dramatically. In 1970 Dr. Clifton Wharton became the first African-American president of a major predominantly White university – Michigan State University in East Lansing. The school was the largest of the state universities, with an enrollment of over 40,000 students. In 1978 he left Michigan State to become chancellor of the nation's largest state university system, that of New York State. In 1976 Dr. Mary Frances Berry became the first African-American woman to head a major White institution of higher learning when she was appointed chancellor of the University of Colorado at Boulder.

In 1967 the median Black family income lagged far behind the national average. By 1989 it had risen to $20,000 – still 60 percent less than that of the average White family. The aggregate buying power of the African-American consumer is now relatively massive: some $270 billion.

LEFT: Winners of the 1993 Essence Awards: (l. to r.) activist Alice Harris, singer/actress Lena Horne, activist Rosa Parks, and U.S. Senator Carol Moseley-Braun (D-Illinois).

BELOW: When the Los Angeles policemen who brutally beat Rodney King were acquitted by a White jury in 1992, massive riots swept the city. One of those who called for a halt to the violence was Rodney King himself.

Black Enterprise Magazine publishes an annual list of the largest Black-owned businesses in the country. Twenty years ago, the Motown Record Company topped the list with sales of $42 million. By 1992 the largest Black business was TLC Beatrice International Holding Company Incorporated, with sales of $1.5 billion.

The question now facing the nation is: How much have we learned from our history? The 1992 riots in Los Angeles after the Rodney King case verdict, which acquitted Los Angeles policemen of brutality to a Black citizen, looked identical to the riots of a previous generation. Once again, the fires kindled by racism and resentment ate away at the fabric of national unity. Almost three decades after the historic civil rights march on Washington, another Black man named King addressed the nation to ask simply, but profoundly, "Can't we all get along?"

The final pages of this book present a photo-gallery of a few of the many contemporary African-Americans who have earned national and international fame for their achievements.

RIGHT: Retired Lakers star Earvin "Magic" Johnson flanked by (l.) Pepsi-Cola chairman Craig Weatherup and *Black Enterprise* editor Earl G. Graves.

BELOW RIGHT: Actress/choreographer/film producer Debbie Allen.

BELOW: Entrepreneur and publisher (*Ebony*, *Jet*, etc.) John H. Johnson.

ABOVE: Businessman, author, and activist Rev. Leon Sullivan.

ABOVE LEFT: Educator, historian, and author John Hope Franklin.

FAR LEFT: Cornel R. West, head of African-American Studies at Princeton University.

LEFT: Professor Henry Gates, the director of the W. E. B. Du Bois Institute for African-American Studies at Harvard University.

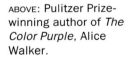ABOVE: Pulitzer Prize-winning author of *The Color Purple*, Alice Walker.

TOP RIGHT: Celebrated novelist and essayist James Baldwin.

RIGHT: Pulitzer Prize-winning poet (and novelist) Rita Dove.

FAR RIGHT: Teacher and poet Gwendolyn Brooks won the first (1950) Putitzer Prize awarded to an African-American.

ABOVE: Pulitzer Prize-winning novelist and editor Toni Morrison.

TOP: Jacob Lawrence's *The Migration of the Negro* (1940-41).

RIGHT: *Family* (1988) by Romare Bearden. Like Lawrence, Bearden often uses aspects of African-American history as subject matter for his canvases.

ABOVE: Army General Colin Powell became the first Black to be made National Security Advisor (1987-89) and then chairman of the Joint Chiefs of Staff (1989-93).

RIGHT: During the 1992 election campaign Governor Bill Clinton and Senator Al Gore lent their support to Senate candidate Carol Moseley-Braun.

ABOVE LEFT: Andrew Young has been a U.S. Congressman, a U.S. ambassador to the U.N., and mayor of Atlanta.

ABOVE: Rev. Jesse Jackson campaigned for the presidential nomination in both 1984 and 1988. Here he addresses delegates at the 1992 Democratic National Convention.

LEFT: Doug Wilder was elected governor of Virginia in 1990.

ABOVE: Wilma Rudolph, the first American woman to win three Olympic medals in track.

ABOVE: 1940s Black pro football stars Marion Motley (l.) and Buddy Young.

LEFT: The immortal Jackie Robinson.

TOP RIGHT: Tennis star Althea Gibson in 1938.

RIGHT: Olympic medalist in track, Florence Griffith Joyner.

ABOVE: Heavyweight champion Joe Louis and Olympic track great Jesse Owen (r.) in 1935.

FAR LEFT, TOP: Former heavyweight champion Sonny Liston with Muhammad Ali.

FAR LEFT, CENTER: Heroic tennis star Arthur Ashe.

FAR LEFT, BOTTOM: Basketball superstar Magic Johnson.

LEFT: Retired Chicago Bulls star Michael Jordan (being fouled).

ABOVE: Fans crowd close to famed saxophonist Charlie Parker (r.) at a jazz festival in Paris in 1949.

TOP RIGHT: Leontyne Price, one of the great operatic sopranos of the twentieth century.

RIGHT: Choreographer Alvin Ailey teaching ballet to a class of blind students.

ABOVE: Legendary blues guitarist B. B. King.

FAR LEFT, TOP: TV superstar Bill Cosby in his role as Cliff Huxtable.

FAR LEFT: Jazz trumpeter Miles Davis.

LEFT: The "Queen of Soul," Aretha Franklin.

ABOVE: Director and actor Spike Lee.

RIGHT: Comedienne and actress Whoopi Goldberg.

FAR RIGHT, TOP: Hattie McDaniel (l.) was the first African-American to win an Oscar, for her role in *Gone With the Wind* (1939).

RIGHT: Actor Denzel Washington plays the title role in the 1992 film *Malcolm X*. It was directed by Spike Lee.

FAR RIGHT, CENTER: Actor Sidney Poitier with the Oscar he won in 1964 for his role in *Lilies of the Field*.

RIGHT: Some principals in the 1991 film *A Rage in Harlem*: (from the left) actor Forrest Whittaker, actress Robin Givens, director Bill Duke, and actor/dancer Gregory Hines.

Index

Page numbers in *italics* indicate illustrations

160